VINTAGE CARS

VINTAGE CARS
Motoring in the 1920s
Cyril Posthumus

Hamlyn
London · New York · Sydney · Toronto

CONTENTS

Acknowledgments The publishers are grateful to the following for the illustrations reproduced in this book:
Autocar; Automobile Manufacturers' Association; Michael Bowler; British Leyland Motor Corporation; British Petroleum; Cadillac; Chrysler; Citroen, l'Editrice dell'Automobile; Fiat; Ford; the Henry Ford Museum; General Motors; Geoffrey Goddard; David Hodges; Indianapolis Motor Speedway; Jaguar; F. Wilson McComb; *Motor*; National Motor Museum; George Oliver; Pamplin Prints; Peugeot; Cyril Posthumus; Press Association; Robin Rew; Rolls-Royce; Rover; Vauxhall; David Burgess Wise.

Published by The Hamlyn Publishing Group Limited
London · New York · Sydney · Toronto
Astronaut House, Feltham, Middlesex, England

ISBN 0 600 39131 0

Printed in Great Britain by Sir Joseph Causton and Sons Limited

THE VINTAGE ERA

When one realises that the motor car has been with us now for almost 90 years, and that the accepted 'Vintage' car era occupies a mere twelve of them, it becomes truly remarkable that it can have so much apparent significance, and arouse so much interest. After much deliberation the Vintage Sports Car Club on its foundation in 1934 agreed the dates of January 1st 1919 and December 31st 1930 as marking the boundaries of production of the kind of cars its members preferred above all. Time has proved the soundness of their choice, and has seen the early amused and slightly incredulous interest shown in their activities kindle into a world-wide following, so that 'they don't make 'em like that any more', uttered with a reverent shake of the head, has become the most hackneyed tribute ever to the workmanship of a bygone age.

'Vintage' is, of course, a wine term in its original sense, defined by Cassells' dictionary as 'the yield of a vineyard or vine district for a particular season', and by Chambers' as 'a season's yield of grapes or wine'. Chambers further adds that a vintage year is 'one in which a particular product (usually wine) reaches an exceptionally high standard'. For year substitute era, and car for wine, and you have the essence of the vintage motoring movement.

The Abbé Dubaquié, a Bordeaux priest, said that 'learning about wine is one of the pleasantest educational pursuits known to man'. Any vintage motorist will say the same for learning about vintage cars, and to judge from the number of books on the subject, writing about them also rates a popular task. This is an attempt to review not just vintage cars, but also the vintage era, to see why it produced such fine, durable motor cars, with qualities which arouse so much interest and admiration over 40 years after they were built.

C.P.

BOOM

'Wanted urgently, immediate or early delivery of new 2-seater car or one little used; good premium paid . . .'

One of 77 'Cars Wanted' advertisements in *The Motor*, February 18, 1920

1919 in the 'land fit for heroes to live in' was a year of delirium. The War was over at last, and while Britain, like every country involved, strove to regain her balance despite an unexpected wave of strikes, unemployment and rocketing prices, hope shone through with persistent brightness. It was all 'san fairy ann' now; things could only get better, was the general feeling, so let us live, laugh, love, spend money, build houses, make things, buy them – all the things we've been short of since 1914 – pots and pans, toys, wheelbarrows, tools, bikes, motorbikes, cars. . . .

Thousands and thousands of young people had been introduced to motor vehicles of some kind or other during the War. They had seen, perhaps ridden in, or driven, the battered Crossleys, Vauxhalls, Sunbeams, Renaults and other makes in anonymous grey or khaki, the ubiquitous Triumph and Douglas motorcycles of the dispatch riders, the massive lumbering tanks, the innumerable lorries – Daimlers, Albions, Leylands, Hallfords, Strakers, Commers, Fords, and so on, and the AEC buses transplanted from the London streets to Flanders mud.

The petrol engine no longer awed or baffled them; instead it attracted, and whereas before the War in humble eyes motor cars were 'for the gentry and not the likes of us', the coming of peace wrought a social revolution and many, many more people dared to want a car; professionals such as commercial travellers saw it as an infinitely more convenient and efficient way of reaching their customers than the train, while others saw in it the means for exploring their own country for the first time.

Simultaneously, countless engineers emerged from a four-year forcing house of armaments manufacture with vast new knowledge of things mechanical and metallurgical. Since 1914 hundreds of factories and their employees had switched willy-nilly from peacetime occupations to turning out munitions, army vehicles, aeroplanes, aero-engines, parts thereof, or some other form of fighting equipment. The wholesale cancellation of war contracts after the Armistice set these new experts free, bursting to put their newfound knowledge into making something useful.

The money was there too; war gratuities, royalties, bonuses and company credits helped to swell the sturdier capital of big, long-established companies in quest of business investments, and all flowed forth in the rosey dawn of peace. In optimistic 1919 the Company Registrar's Office was a grossly overworked Government department, and it was tragically ironic that much of this pressure of work would so soon be transferred to the bankruptcy courts.

New names

The motor trade geared up for business. Existing car manufacturers such as Wolseley, Austin, Vauxhall, Daimler, Rolls-Royce, Humber, Singer and many others cleared their factories of war work and prepared to build motor cars again, while many completely new names, and some strange permutations of old ones, appeared. Armstrong Siddeley sprang from a union between Siddeley-Deasy and Armstrong-Whitworth, while three long-established marques in Sunbeam, Talbot and Darracq created a new Anglo-French combine, STD Ltd.

The number of new British makes was staggering –

Spacious days, when one could park at any angle and look at one's engine without being hustled along. The 'bobby' looks placidly on, while an august sleeve-valve Daimler and an interesting American friction-drive Trumbull cyclecar pass by. The car in trouble is a Standard.

there were over 40 of them, with names such as Bean, Cubitt, Guy, Seabrook, Ruston-Hornsby, Cluley, Clyno, Dawson, Enfield-Allday, Beardmore, Cooper, Charron-Laycock, Westwood and many, many more. Standing out amongst them were Bentley, Alvis, Aston Martin and Leyland, but these are only notable in hindsight as they typify the Vintage car at its best. Many cars were humbler in specification and price, some offered dull but worthy value, and others contributed as little to automobile design and aesthetics as the much despised cars of the 1930s and the 'bulboids' of the first decade after the Second World War.

The great aim was to build cars, any cars, to meet the new demand. It was a lot easier then to set up as a motor manufacturer with limited capital. No enormously costly jigs and tooling were required, or vast hydraulic presses to form complex steel body panels in one operation; there was no pressure die-casting of intricate components, no plastics for interior mouldings or delicate electrical parts, no printed electronic circuits. Quantity or 'mass production' was still a transAtlantic practice rather

looked down upon, and although forward-thinking companies like Morris, Fiat, Renault, and the new French marque, Citroen, planned to emulate the Americans, there was still plenty of room for the smaller car maker with traditional methods.

Getting started

Capital to acquire or rent a small factory, to buy initial parts, materials and tools, and to pay workers' wages were the prior needs. Once the cars got rolling, the money should roll too. Wood, steel, bronze, brass, copper and aluminium were the basic materials in the car of the 1920s, and its most basic specification comprised a separate channel steel chassis, a front-mounted engine more often with side valves than overhead, a three- or four-speed crash-type gearbox, sometimes in unit, often still separate from the engine, a 'live' rigid rear axle, a beam front axle, two-wheel brakes, $\frac{1}{4}$, $\frac{1}{2}$ or $\frac{3}{4}$ elliptic or cantilever leaf springs, artillery or disc wheels, and a separately mounted body of wood-cum-metal-cum fabric.

A firm could buy chassis members from heavy presswork specialists such as Rubery Owen or Mechans, springs and axles from experts such as Jonas Woodhead, engines from Dorman, Coventry Simplex, Coventry Climax, Meadows, Alpha or other specialists, and gearboxes from Moss, Wrigleys or David Brown Ltd. Clutches, radiators, magnetos, carburettors, steering gear, brakes, even mudguards, were all purchasable provided there was the cash or the *bona fides* for a credit account. Thus many, but

It took all sorts to make a Vintage world. Left: a 1920 photograph of a Fiat 9 litre four-cylinder 50-60 Tipo 5, built for armoured car use in the First World War by the company's American licensees, but fitted with post-war British limousine bodywork. Note the ornate roof rack with second spare wheel, the wood-spoked artillery wheels, and the fact that the chauffeur had presumably to reach his seat from the left, with that spare wheel impeding offside entry.

Below, left: at the other end of the motoring scale came the humble but ubiquitous Model T Ford which brought motoring to the masses. This one, seen in a Surrey street in 1920, has left hand drive, 'mixed' front tyres, oil scuttle lamps, electric head and side lights, an unusual registration number and prominent AA badge. Specification included a 2·9 litre four-cylinder side-valve engine, two-speed epicycle gearbox, and transverse leaf springing front and rear. Rough, tough, cheap and versatile, the T was the world's first true people's car, and over 15 million were built between 1909 and 1927.

Below: Henry Ford's Model T figures again in this evocative English country scene featuring divers means of transport and pleasure. That wet, unmade road, stirred up by hooves, gig wheels and car tyres, will soon be pretty mucky underneath.

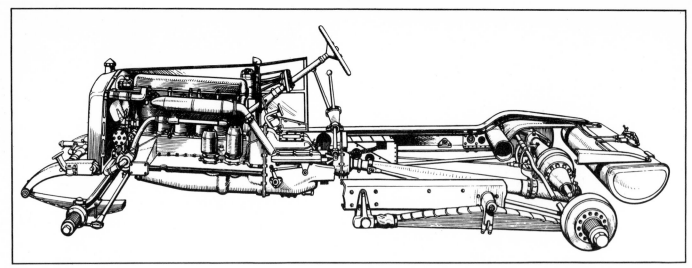

fortunately not all, of the post-war newcomers among motor manufacturers were little more than assemblers of outside-supplied components. Such firms mushroomed, not only in Britain but in France (where at least 50 new marques came into being), Italy and even defeated Germany, where a surprising number of new makes had a brief shoestring existence before the collapse of the Deutschmark killed many off.

The true seed

But the true Vintage seed lay in a higher quality market. Fortunately there were conscientious new designers who were not content with a characterless hodge-podge of bought-out parts, who wanted to make their own engines, transmissions and frames the way *they* felt they should be made, and who managed to find enough backing to produce their ideal cars. W.O. Bentley and his famous 3 litre sports car is the obvious British example, although the finances of the Bentley company were almost always precarious.

Such designers wanted better performance than the average proprietary engine of the time could offer,

This Sheffield-Simplex chassis (above) cost over four times the price of the Austin Twenty (below) in 1921 – yet both nearly bankrupted their respective manufacturers. At £2250 the Sheffield-Simplex chassis offered a huge 7·7 litre side-valve engine with six separate cylinders, four speed gearbox, cantilever rear spring and optional front brakes. At £2700 with bodywork the cars proved too costly, and only a switch to motor cycle manufacture saved the company.

Right: *Just as they do today, Chevrolet marketed an overhead valve V8 back in 1918. But despite its proclaimed advantages, this earlier enterprise was not continued for long.*

The Austin Twenty had a sound, simple, 3·6 litre four-cylinder monobloc engine and four-speed gearbox, and cost £550 for the chassis or £695 for the open tourer. It was Austin's only model in 1921, a policy which proved disastrous, and only the introduction of the famous Twelve sent the receivers packing and saved the make.

and obtained it by designing their own units with overhead valves, sturdy bottom ends, proper lubrication, and better balance of reciprocating parts. If they had to compromise and use other people's engines they improved them where possible, with the reservation that, once soundly established, they would build their own.

Their chassis might be pressed and rivetted together for them by an outside firm, but they would design it themselves for correct weight distribution and rigidity, with the correct length and strength of the springs, rather than compromise with what was available 'off the shelf'. W.O.Bentley and his design team designed every single item on the 3 litre except the Rudge Whitworth wire wheels, the carburettors and magnetos, and the steering wheel. As they had no machine shop or foundry the manufacture of parts had to be sub-contracted. In his autobiography, Bentley wrote: 'We had to have *everything* made; gearbox, clutch, differential, bearings, stub axles – everything', but this was because the Bentley was *designed* from the very start, and another's gearbox or transmission or axle would not do for 'W.O.'. It cost Bentley Motors much money, but it paid off in performance and longevity.

Moving to the top of the price scale into the large luxury car class, designers were more able to give their ideas full rein without inhibitions about cost. Parry Thomas evolved the Leyland Eight, a remarkable design with many features ahead of its day,

Hispano-Suiza of France, fresh from building thousands of successful aero-engines, introduced their magnificent overhead camshaft sixes with four wheel servo-assisted brakes, while Isotta-Fraschini, of Italy, already old hands at four wheel brakes but rich in wartime engine experience too, built Europe's first production straight eight.

From air to ground

The end of the war in the air brought other famous names in aviation down to earth and on to the road; the Avro was a short-lived British make, there were Voisin, Farman, Bleriot, and others from France, Maybach and Rumpler from Germany, Ansaldo from Italy, and Duesenberg and Rickenbacker from the United States. None of these newcomers, advanced though many of their cars were, ruffled the old-established quality manufacturers such as Rolls-Royce, Daimler, Napier and Lanchester, while Mercedes of Stuttgart stood like a rock 'midst the German financial quicksands, marketing a range of cars little changed at first from their 1914 models. Other marques concerned with getting into production quickly likewise revived their pre-war designs rather than rush untried new models. The demand was such that, new or old fashioned, there seemed to be plenty of room for all in those blithe early post-war months.

Problems – and a Motor Show

Despite the intense fervour to produce that swept Britain, the Continent and the USA, somehow the

Gallic grace, epitomised by this glorious Paris-built 32CV, 6·6 litre six-cylinder overhead camshaft Hispano-Suiza cabriolet of 1923. This highly revered luxury make originated in Spain with a Swiss designer, hence the name.

fine flow of glossy new cars from factory to customer, uppermost in so many manufacturers' minds, was very slow to materialise. In Britain a series of strikes on the railways, in the coal mines and other vital services strangled the flow of supplies from the foundries and factories. Supplies of cheap steel, much in demand, became erratic, while a serious moulders' strike added to difficulties. The production of frames, axles, engines, wheels and other components lagged further and further behind orders, and while unskilled labour was plentiful there were design staff shortages. Advertisements for fine new cars began to contain apologies for delayed deliveries.

In the middle of it came the first post-war Motor Show at Olympia, in November 1919. There had not been a Show since 1913, and the ill-ventilated halls were crammed as never before with the wares of the British motor industry, and with the British public in unprecedented numbers. They flocked to Olympia, though recently chided for "squandermania" by a Government facing a £500 million Budget deficit, to see a record 272 different makes of car, including 134 British, 78 French, 15 Italian and 42 American. They saw the new Bentley without knowing that parts of its engine were made of wood, a remarkable Straker-Squire with overhead camshaft six-cylinder engine highly redolent of aircraft practice, a fantastic Enfield-Allday with five-cylinder air-cooled radial engine, an equally fantastic Cosmos with three-cylinder radial engine, a clean, competent aluminium six-cylinder engine with wet liners by AC, many other sound but often uninteresting models, and a whole clutch of spidery cyclecars.

The public came to draughty Olympia in such volume that at times the doors had to be closed on them, order books were filled and double filled, and optimism reigned. All that was needed was the cars. As 1920 came in and the orders were not fulfilled, customers became restless. Prices were rising all the time, and the man who ordered an '11·9' at £300 at the Show found himself obliged to pay £450 six months later, or forfeit his order. Any new car available for 'immediate delivery' was rare and highly suspect, and most agents advertised cars as 'on view' and could not guarantee delivery dates.

Meantime prewar cars sold like hot cakes at inflated prices. A 1914 Calthorpe costing £168 new commanded £475 secondhand early in 1920, a 1913 Rolls-Royce costing £1,240 new sold for £7,200, the 'modern' trick of paying a premium on top of the retail price for a much desired model was widely practised, and many advertisements asked "What offers?". And all the time the American cars poured

British solidarity. Though lacking the Hispano's elegance the Leyland luxury car embodied many advanced features, including a straight-eight overhead camshaft engine, servo-assisted brakes and torsion bar-assisted suspension.

in, despite having to pay the McKenna duty of $33\frac{1}{3}$ per cent imposed on all imported cars at that time. Ford assembled Model Ts at Manchester, thereby avoiding the tax, and offered matchless value, but other American cars, always good on power and comfort if not on fuel economy, sold as fast as they entered the showrooms – well known makes such as Oldsmobiles, Chevrolets, Buicks and Overlands, and interesting rarer ones such as Apperson, Maibohm, Dort, Columbian etc.

France had her problems, too, suffering a severe shortage of coal, not through strikes but because most of her mines were in the war-stricken northern areas and had been flooded or badly damaged. No coal meant no electricity, and many factories could not work properly, if at all. Many foundries, also in the battle areas, were disabled, and this set car production schedules many months back, further aggravated by the introduction of an 8 hour working day and, as in Britain, steeply rising prices. Italy was even worse off, being in the throes of political turmoil; rocketing costs of food brought riots in the cities, and raw materials, always scarce south of the Alps, were extremely costly.

Meeting the market

Despite all the difficulties, cars were built somehow; not enough to meet feverish demand, but some. Long-established concerns fared best, with parts and material suppliers giving them preference over unknown new firms. On the other hand, determined newcomers with a wealth of war-bred ingenuity could often improvise more easily. Some early postwar cyclecars were virtually hand built, while firms like Alvis, who insisted on doing their own designing, got their first cars running before some others over-dependent on outside suppliers.

OWEN MAGNETIC

Banishing the Commonplace

THOSE who are distinguished for their Owen Magnetic Motor Cars are strict individualists, though not bizarre.

Their town and country houses, their gardens, all their possessions are far from the commonplace.

And so when it comes to a car, they insist on getting away from the monotonous. Up and down the Avenue, or at the Opera, or at the Country Club—wherever the world of fashion congregates—certain cars distinguish the vivid personalities from the drab.

Each Owen Magnetic expresses this idea of unobtrusive elegance. Exterior and interior colors and upholstering are decided upon by the owner.

All the appointments show careful selections—such as the silver hardware, the lighting fixtures, the carpeting.

The most casual observer knows instantly that the owner is a person of faultless taste.

Just as The Owen banishes the commonplace in appearance, so does it eliminate the mechanical crudities of yesteryear. At the touch of finger-tip this great car is in complete control—giant power leaps across an air space from engine to wheels. No gear shifting—no clanking noises—no jerks nor lunges—just a quiet, floating sensation, entirely different!

Attractive brochure, adequately describing the Owen Magnetic, will be mailed upon request.

THE BAKER, RAUCH & LANG CO., CLEVELAND, OHIO

Also Builders of Rauch & Lang Electrics and Custom Coach Bodies of Quality

Metropolitan Distributors

OWEN MAGNETIC MOTOR SALES CORP.

Broadway at 57th St., New York

American design was much less stereotyped half a century ago. This 1919 car had a six-cylinder petrol engine generating current which actuated the Entz magnetic transmission – smooth, silent and flexible, but expensive.

As 1920 advanced the supply problems eased and production figures rose. Prices, however, followed suit implacably (petrol had already gone up 8d per gallon in February). In February 1920 a 22hp four cylinder four-seater Model T Ford tourer with self starter and lighting sold at £250, an 11·9 Bean tourer cost £550, a Phoenix two-seater £450, a Belsize £640 (without electric starter) and an Arrol-Johnston £625. By October of that year all these prices had risen a further 6 to 10 per cent, yet the Ford, the 'old Tin Lizzie' which was the butt of so much humour, still sold at under £300. There was bitterness as well as derision in the round of Ford jokes and rhymes, epitomised by:

"Bitza tin, bitza board,
Put together make a Ford"

and

"What's the time when two Fords
pass each other? Tin past tin".

The homely Model T rose above such quips; it gave reliable transport to thousands and thousands, and clearly Britain would have to do something about it pretty soon.

BURSTING BUBBLES

'By order of the Receiver . . . for sale as a
going concern, the very valuable,
modern and completely equipped
Briton Motor Works . . . together
with the entire contents . . . and
the designs and rights of
manufacture of the
Briton car . . .'

Advertisement in *The Autocar*,
January 1922

As the spring of 1920 advanced into summer, motor manufacturers became increasingly worried. Having overcome production problems and got the new cars flowing off the lines at last, they found the orders just were not coming in. The high cost of living and the ever-rising prices were to blame. The first cloud had come in April when Bank rate was raised to 7 per cent, and in ensuing months it became clear that, much as the public might desire new cars, they just could not afford them, even with hire purchase aids. Trade fell off all round, factories had to put off workers, and unemployment rose to over a million; the bubble had burst, and the fine new boom gave way to unexpected recession.

It was much the same elsewhere, with the United States motor industry suffering in particular, and many smaller makers closing down, Germany was in the financial doldrums, and France decided not to hold her Paris Salon in 1920. Britain's Motor Show duly took place, however, attracting so many exhibitors that it had to be split into two, one half at Olympia, the other at White City, while even then several makes abstained from the Show. In all there were 149 British makes (50 years later only 31 existed!), and 67 French, 50 American, 18 Italian and 8 Belgian makes (the Germans were not allowed to exhibit). There were no startling novelties like radial engines this time, but an enormous variety of vehicles ranging from cyclecars costing £200 or so to super-luxury limousines selling at over £3,000. But the buying spree was over, and cars were hard to sell.

The gloom deepened with the coming, on January 1st 1921, of a revised and more expensive method of car taxation. Since 1910 this had been based on the RAC horsepower formula, assessed on the bore but not the stroke of the engine and the number of cylinders, with a sliding scale of charges according to the horsepower, plus a petrol tax payable by all. Under the new system, tax was raised to £1 per RAC horsepower, and the petrol tax repealed. Most motorists would have preferred a straight petrol tax, but the authorities decreed otherwise.

Long strokes

The result was a spate of cheap light cars with 'tax dodging' engines which had narrow bores and long strokes, exaggerated by one critic as "the bore of a threepenny bit and the stroke of an overgrown alpenstock", and a serious fall in sales of big cars and those

This 1921 Southport-built Vulcan 12 had a 1·8 litre side-valve four cylinder Dorman engine and four speeds.

with unfavourable cylinder dimensions. The Model T Ford and American imported cars, all with biggish engines and large bores, were notable sufferers.

A yardstick of the times was provided by Morris, who had produced 276 cars in September 1920 but only 74 in January 1921. Other firms were worse hit, and several small ones went to the wall through lack of finance. Vulcan, Briton, even the Austin Motor Co., had the receivers in. Austin came close to being taken over by an American firm, although happily the company was quickly refloated, to make a significant contribution to future motoring history.

Another drawback of the £1 per horsepower tax was that the new small-bore light cars it encouraged were not wanted overseas, where conditions were tougher, and in 1921 British car exports dropped over 45 per cent compared with 1920. Of course exports were not then vital to the country's survival as they are nowadays, and the 1921 total was a mere 3,800 cars, compared with 721,094 in 1971!

The solution, although not everyone saw it, was to cut prices. It is traditional to cite William R. Morris as the bold, farsighted manufacturer whose sensational cuts in February 1921 showed the British industry the

way to go, but in fact he was comfortably preceded by Swift and Bean, who made respective reductions of £55 and £105 in September 1920, and in the next few months by Vauxhall, ABC, GWK, Citroen, Daimler, Westwood, Albert, Jowett and Singer.

When Morris followed suit, his biggest cut was £100 on the Cowley four-seater, bringing it down from £525 to £425. Less daring makers announced guarantees against reductions, or promised to refund any differences on orders received and paid for, but in the end they all had to conform and reduce their prices. Morris certainly followed up spectacularly, with another £81 cut on the Cowley in mid-1921, and another of £74 just before the 1922 Motor Show, thereby reducing its purchase price by more than half, from £525 to £225, within two years, and keeping his factory humming busily.

The cyclecar craze

Meantime the quest for the most car for the least money took more than one form. Cheapest and often nastiest of all was the cyclecar, that precarious compromise between motorcycle and car, of which a French journal remarked despairingly when reviewing several: "the cyclecar always follows catas-

Cyclecars 'of infinite varietie'. Above: the 1920 AV Monocar with rear-mounted side-valve twin-cylinder engine, wire and bobbin steering and centre-pivot front axle, which won a cyclecar race at Brooklands at 59mph. Left: Edwardian though it appears, this Elfe cyclecar is competing in a 1922 French hillclimb. Driver and passenger sat in tandem, ahead of a narrow-angle vee-twin engine.
Below: the 1921 Tamplin with tandem seating, front-mounted JAP engine, belt drive and elegant wheel discs.

trophes!''. The breed was no post-war invention; the craze began after an earlier recession in 1910, with the amazing French Bédélia and the more rational British GN, built by two ultra-enthusiasts in H.R. Godfrey and A. Frazer Nash. These cars were soon supplemented by others, mostly employing twin-cylinder motorcycle engines and belt, friction, chain or, more rarely, shaft final drive in spidery chassis with rudimentary springing and steering.

Production had been interrupted during the War, but when peace returned, so did the cyclecar, the prime motives of cost-saving and lightness bringing both ingenuity and optimism. The Carden had its flat-twin two-stroke engine at the rear, geared direct to the axle through two speeds, had the skimpiest of wire wheels and minimal but well-shaped two-seater bodywork. The name Blériot, famous in aviation, appeared on two widely differing cyclecars, one from the French parent company having a two-stroke, two-cylinder engine and shaft drive, whereas the British off-shoot, called the Whippet, had a fierce 998cc vee-twin Blackburne unit driving the rear wheels through

17

British 'dependables'. The 1261cc Wolseley Ten (left) of the early Vintage era was distinguished by its shaft-driven sohc engine which gave it quite a lively performance. Suspension was by quarter-elliptics front and rear, and the transmission comprised a three-speed gearbox on the rear axle with worm final-drive. The dashboard is typically Vintage, featuring a 60mph speedometer, ammeter, clock and fuel gauge.

Above: *epitomising the solid middle class family car was the Vintage Humber 15·9, powered by a 2·8 litre four-cylinder side-valve engine. Most Humbers were finished in dull but seemingly indestructible beige or khaki.*

a Zenith Gradua variable gear and belt drive – a sort of pioneer DAF.

Another noted flying personality dabbling briefly in cyclecars was Grahame-White, who produced an American-style "Buckboard" which was little more than a platform supporting a 350cc Precision engine, two-speed gearbox and chain drive, and one seat. The Tamplin initially aped the prewar Bédélia, its cen-

trally-mounted twin-cylinder JAP engine driving the rear wheels through three speeds and yards of belt, and its seats being in tandem; later the makers re-thought it, moved the engine forward and the seats sideways, and adopted chain drive, while the body became distinctly sporting in polished aluminium.

Best of them all was the GN, which had a lusty over-1000cc 90-degree vee-twin air-cooled engine driving the rear wheels through four separate chains and sprockets, each with dog clutches, giving three forward speeds and reverse. The frame was a simple rectangular affair of channel steel, springing was by four quarter-elliptics, one at each corner, the body was a two-seater of rakish aspect, and total weight was a mere 6½cwt for the "Popular" model. Fiercer variants, the Legère and the Vitesse, had overhead valves and aluminium pistons. GNs were raced very successfully for several years.

Other cyclecars included the Richardson, Metro-Tyler and Douglas, the Duo and Benjamin from France, and a number from Germany, while of three-wheelers the Morgan was, of course, the most famous,

More cyclecars. *Archie Frazer Nash (above)* ascending
the Brooklands test hill in a GN Vitesse, circa 1920.
Power came from a 1087cc 90 degree air-cooled vee-twin
overhead-valve engine set across the bonnet and driving
the solid rear axle through chains and clutched sprockets.

rivalled for a time by New Hudson, d'Yrsan, Omega,
LSD and TB. One gets what one pays for, however.
None of the cyclecars mentioned cost more than
£200, some considerably less, and standards of comfort, weather protection and reliability were never
very high. One needed to be a fair mechanic to get the
best out of them, while good nerves and a spartan
indifference to noise and vibration also helped.

Small cars

Contemporary with the cyclecar was the small car,
costing up to £100 more, but offering better protection, a quieter, more comfortable ride, less main-
tenance and greater dependability. Most of them were
scaled down editions of large, conventional cars, with
front-mounted engine and shaft drive to the rear
wheels. Engines varied from the air-cooled transverse twin of the Rover Eight to the similar but water-
cooled unit of the Yorkshire-built Jowett, the 90-
degree twin-cylinder, oil-cooled Belsize-Bradshaw,

and the higher performance overhead valve flat-twin
sporting ABC, to a choice of proprietary four-cylinder
side valve units and the neat little 970cc overhead
valve engine of the 1921 Talbot 8/18.

Some cars were utilitarian offshoots of prestige
makes – the Stoneleigh by Armstrong Siddeley, for
example, the Buckingham by Alvis, the Stellite by
Wolseley, and the remarkable 10hp Trojan introduced by Leyland in mid-1922. This was a true utility
device with four-cylinder water-cooled two-stroke
engine under the seat, duplex chain drive through a
two-speed epicyclic gear, full cantilever springing

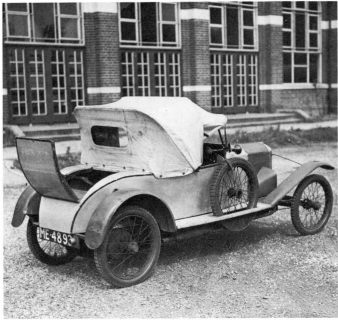

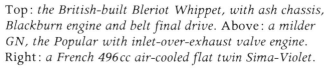

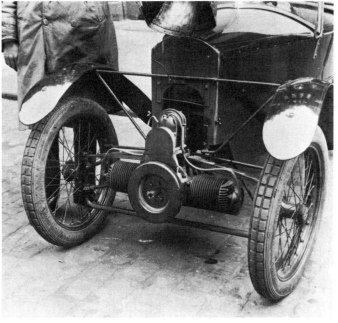

Top: *the British-built Bleriot Whippet, with ash chassis, Blackburn engine and belt final drive.* Above: *a milder GN, the Popular with inlet-over-exhaust valve engine.* Right: *a French 496cc air-cooled flat twin Sima-Violet.*

and solid tyres. This virtually foolproof and indestructible car was built until 1930, practically unchanged apart from optional pneumatic tyres and other refinements, its totally unbecoming exterior being offset by remarkable slow-but-sure dependability, which attracted a clientele of similar nature.

A new miniature car from France was the Peugeot Quadrilette, a successor to the delightful little prewar Bébé designed by Ettore Bugatti. The Quadrilette had a four-cylinder, fixed-head, side-valve engine of only 680cc, with crankshaft running in ball bearings, transverse leaf front springs, quarter-elliptics at the rear, and three-speed gearbox on the rear axle. Its

bodywork began in 1920 as a narrow tandem two-seater, but became more conventional as time passed, acquiring more comfort and weight, necessitating a bigger engine. Another French bestseller was the 856cc 5CV Citroen, the famous "Cloverleaf" three-seater introduced in 1922 with quarter-elliptic springs all round and disc wheels.

Germany built her *kleinwagen* too, the Hanomag introduced in 1924. Of modern but austere concept, it had a rear-mounted 499cc overhead valve single-cylinder water-cooled engine driving by chain through a three-speed gearbox to the narrow rear axle. The body was integral with the platform chassis, front suspension was independent, and the car, nicknamed the *Kommisbrot* (Army loaf) because of its shape, was uniquely advanced in having a full-width "envelope" body with no running boards. There was a single headlight set flush in the rounded nose. Like the Model T Ford, this little 40mph car costing the

German miniature: the 1924 Hanomag 'Kommisbrot' with full-width body and rear-mounted 499cc overhead valve engine.

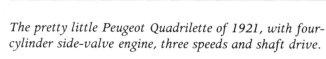

The pretty little Peugeot Quadrilette of 1921, with four-cylinder side-valve engine, three speeds and shaft drive.

equivalent of under £100 had to endure lighthearted jingles such as the German equivalent of:

"As only tin and paint are used,
The Hanomag is soon produced."

Nonetheless, 15,775 were built in open and closed forms, between 1924 and 1928.

Italy contributed an appealing little *microvettura* called the Temperino, which first appeared in 1919–20 with an 1010cc overhead inlet valve, air-cooled vee-twin engine behind a conventional front, driving through a three-speed gearbox and propellor shaft to the right rear wheel only. A girder-type chassis was braced by a cast aluminium bulkhead, and suspension was by three-quarter elliptic leaf springs at the front and quarter elliptics at the rear. In 1922 a side-valve monobloc vertical twin engine of 1021cc was

fitted, and these little cars were built at Turin at the rate of seven per day, in two- and four-seater, and even taxi forms, until 1925.

The true miniature car clearly appealed to Italian engineers, for others built and sold in appreciable numbers in the vintage era included the shaft-driven FIAM with 706cc air-cooled vertical twin engine, produced from 1921 to 1926, and also made under licence in Hungary as the Manfred-Weiss, and the SAM of 1924–28 with 882cc four cylinder side-valve engine and shaft drive. The FOD of 1924–27 had a 565cc overhead valve four-cylinder water-cooled engine forming part of a very neat combined chassis/body

Every British road saw this car, the reliable, inexpensive and highly popular 11·9 'Bullnose' Morris Cowley.

Cutaway drawing of Britain's most famous 'baby', the immortal Austin Seven with four cylinders, three speeds, shaft drive, and four wheel brakes, introduced in 1922.

structure of steel and aluminium, and weighed less than 1,000 lb. Several hundred of these little cars were made in open and closed two-seater forms.

Austin's wonderful Seven

Undoubtedly the most important of all new 'baby' cars was the Austin Seven, a true miniature of large car practice, owing nothing to the cyclecar. As introduced at the 1922 Motor Show, it had a 696 cc four-cylinder side-valve water-cooled engine in unit with a three-speed gearbox, mounted in an A-shaped frame formed of two longitudinal members and cross bracing, and driving the rear wheels by shaft. Four wheel brakes were fitted, and springing was by transverse leaf at the front, and quarter-elliptics at

the rear. The little car was only 8 ft 10 in in length, and with a light open four-seater body the first Seven weighed a mere 7 cwt, could attain 50 mph, was economical, reliable, easy to drive and, as time was to prove, remarkably durable.

It went into production at Longbridge the following year with engine enlarged to 747 cc and equipped with an electric starter supplementing the handle. In addition to the four-seater Chummy, open two-seater and saloon versions became available as time passed. Costing only £165 in 1923, the wonderful little Austin Seven proved immensely popular, and some 400,000 were built between 1923 and 1938, when production ceased.

This Italian Temperino miniature four-seater of 1922 had a 1021 cc vertical-twin engine driving one rear wheel only.

Dixi of Germany, later BMW, built the Austin Seven under licence; this is their 1928 3/15PS model.

The Seven was built under licence in France as the Rosengart, in Germany as the Dixi – the car which ended the career of the Hanomag *Kommisbrot* and later became the BMW – in Japan as the Datsun, and in the United States as the Bantam. It also served as a van, and even as a military vehicle, and was raced extensively with enormous success. Its little four cylinder engine was subsequently made in modified form by Reliant from 1939 to 1963, Austin having sold them the design rights for use in their commercial and Regal passenger three-wheelers. These Reliant-built Austin units are still being raced today in 750 Motor Club Formula events – a remarkable testimony to a fifty year old design.

The Austin Seven in Britain, and the Citroen, Peugeot and Mathis – an 8 hp side-valve four-cylinder, four-speed model – in France, virtually killed off the cyclecar class by 1924–25, for their refinements cost scarcely £50 more once large scale production was under way. Thus motor car design had 'jelled' within six years of the Armistice into a front-mounted, water-cooled engine, rear shaft-driven rut – but it was a broad rut, permitting many interesting permutations in the size of cylinders, choice of materials, type of valve gear and transmission, wheels and body. Within these bounds lay splendid variety for the imaginative designer to practice his art. Inevitably, though, there were the non-conformists who broke away in their quest for perfection.

The strange ones
There was, for example, that Cosmos seen at Olympia in 1919, with a front-mounted three-cylinder, 1200 cc overhead valve air-cooled radial engine like a miniature aircraft unit. Small wonder, since it was the work of A.H.R. (later Sir Roy) Fedden, who had been with Straker-Squire and then with the Bristol Aeroplane Co. His car had suspension by bell cranks compressing on large transverse coil springs and pressed steel wheels; it weighed only 6 cwt with a light and very ugly open body. Unfortunately the unorthodox always needs more money for development, and the Cosmos project ran out of capital before the car could be put into production at a proclaimed rate of 200 per week at 200 guineas per car.

Still more complex was the Enfield-Allday "Bullet" at the same Show. This had a 1,247 cc five-cylinder

Out of its time – the 1922 North-Lucas with rear-mounted radial engine, rear swing axles and inboard brakes.

radial engine with rod-operated "cuff" (i.e., short sleeve) valves; it was enclosed by a cowling into which cooling air was forced by fan blades on the flywheel. This engine was installed at the front of a triangulated frame of small tubes, with cantilever leaf springs all round. Designers were A.W. Reeves and A.C. Bertelli, later of Aston Martin fame. The "Bullet", like the Cosmos, rated as an early "dream car", for it never reached production.

More shattering still was the 1922 North-Lucas. This also had a five-cylinder air-cooled radial engine, utilising JAP motorcycle cylinders, which was mounted horizontally over the rear axle and drove down through a three-speed gearbox and swing axles. Suspension was independent to all four wheels

Successful unorthodoxy was practised by Tatra of Czechoslovakia in the flat-twin engined, backbone-framed T12.

The chassis of the remarkable Enfield-Allday 'Bullet' with five-cylinder radial engine. This car was one of the sensations of the 1919 Olympia Motor Show.

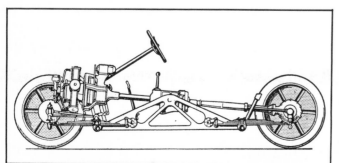

Dr Edmund Rumpler, famous German aircraft designer in the First World War, applied aeronautical theories to an automobile with this surprising result. The Rumpler which appeared at the 1921 Berlin Show has a mid-located six-cylinder 'W' engine, independent rear suspension and unusual streamlined bodywork. The cars were costly to construct and disappeared after 1926. The engine/transmission unit of the Rumpler (right), with its cylinders in three banks of two, three-speed gearbox and independent swing axles was years ahead of its time.

by swinging arms and coil springs enclosing hydraulic dampers – a remarkable early anticipation of the modern 'coaxial' system. Rear brakes were mounted inboard, and the body was of integral construction, formed in aluminium over an ash frame. There was inter-axle seating and the roof had a large translucent panel of doped aeroplane fabric to admit light. Designers were O.D. North, later Scammell's chief designer, and Ralph Lucas. The one car built cost about £2,500, was sold in around 1935 for £5, and later, alas, was scrapped.

A novel Italian design was the San Giusto, which first appeared at the 1922 Milan Show. Designed by Dr Ucelli, it had a 748cc four-cylinder pressure air-cooled engine mounted just ahead of the rear axles in a square-section backbone chassis, and driving through a combined four-speed gearbox and differential unit, as on a modern racing car. Transverse leaf springs and wishbones gave all-round independent suspension, there were four-wheel brakes and wire wheels, and the whole car was beautifully engineered. But it was too heavy for that little engine, besides being costly to produce, and did not survive beyond 1925.

A backbone frame, but of tubular type, also featured on the Czech-built Tatra T12 light car which

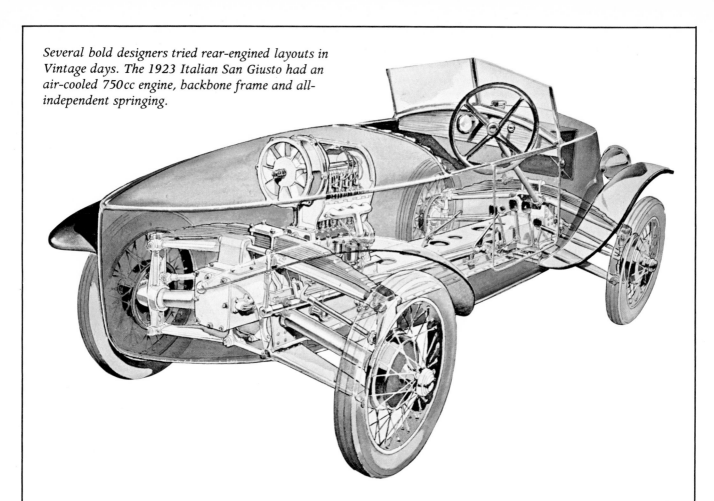

Several bold designers tried rear-engined layouts in Vintage days. The 1923 Italian San Giusto had an air-cooled 750cc engine, backbone frame and all-independent springing.

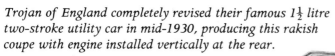

Trojan of England completely revised their famous 1½ litre two-stroke utility car in mid-1930, producing this rakish coupe with engine installed vertically at the rear.

The 1930 Burney Streamline had its 3 litre straight-eight twin-cam engine at the extreme rear, all-round independent suspension, and composite chassis/body construction.

made its debut at the Prague Show of 1923. Designed by Hans Ledwinka, it had a 1,056cc air-cooled flat-twin six-valve engine/gearbox unit forming the front end of the backbone, with the propeller shaft passing inside the tube to the rear swing axles. A special two-pinion, two-bevel final drive dispensed with universal joints, and this feature survived on Tatra cars and trucks for over 40 years. At first, front suspension was by a transverse leaf and beam axle, but later this was changed to divided axles, making the T12 all-independently sprung and admirably suited to rugged Eastern European roads of the 1920s. Unlike most unorthodox designs, this one endured for many years.

In impoverished Germany, too, novel and ingenious designs appeared. One-time aircraft designer Dr Rumpler stole the 1921 Berlin Show with his remarkable automobile embodying aircraft principles. Its 2·6 litre engine had six cylinders disposed in 'W' fashion (i.e., in three banks of two cylinders, like a broad arrow). This compact unit was mounted ahead of the rear wheels, driving back through a three-speed gearbox and rear swing axles. The springing medium all round was long cantilever springs, the steering was installed centrally in the nose of the streamlined hull, and there were flat metal mudguards mounted horizontally. Open and closed versions were built, but the Rumpler was too revolutionary and expensive to last beyond 1926.

This all too often was the fate of unorthodoxy. Apart from an extrovert minority, motorists as a whole, of any generation, show a strong resistance to the out-of-the-ordinary in motor cars. They would select the de Luxe model for a few extra pounds, then as now, to show the Joneses they could afford it, but basically their car had to be like everyone else's. In America, where already in the 1920s automobiles

were taken for granted as mere transportation, this instinct was strong, and the manufacturer who strayed from convention had little chance of survival.

A highly interesting 'probe' into future design, however, was the Martin Aerodynamic, designed in 1926 by J.V.Martin and General 'Billy' Mitchell of General Motors. It had a rear-mounted engine, front radiator, independent suspension all round by aero-elastic, a tubular frame of aircraft type (in effect a spaceframe), and a fully streamlined all-aluminium body that was well beyond vintage 'context'. The underneath was completely sealed off, and a speed of 110mph was reported. Plans for production fell through, for reasons unknown.

Aeronautical practice also figured prominently in the 'one-off' American Martin Aerodynamic, built in 1927. It had a rear engine, aero-elastic all-independent suspension, tubular space frame chassis, and fully streamlined all-aluminium bodywork, with a passenger compartment resembling an aircraft cabin.

THE WAYAHEAD

'Save ten steps a day for each of twelve
thousand employees, and you will have saved
fifty miles of wasted motion and
misspent energy'.

Henry Ford

As the early post-war ferments settled down to a more stabilised peace, car production got going in real earnest. Methods of building a car in those days depended on the number being produced and the class of car. The relatively small output manufacturer could not use extensively mechanised forms of production and relied to a surprising extent on hand work. The engine, transmission and chassis might be bought out as separate items, but they still had to be put together. Obviously fixtures or templates were used for siting and drilling important holes and locating key parts, but a car is a complicated affair to assemble, and the skilled engineering craftsman came into his own.

Parts might be forged or cast, but they still had to be 'fettled' or cleaned up, and there was a great deal of hand fitting demanding considerable skill. The portable electric drill so common today was a clumsy and rare thing at that time, and the hand wheel-brace, generally termed a 'gut buster', was an essential tool in small factories. A good 'hand' and 'eye' in shrewdly weighing, feeling and seeing the correctness of a part still counted as much as a micrometer or vernier in many workshops, a good fitter had to know how to file flat and radiused surfaces, and to shape metal into various forms for brackets, clips and a dozen other functions. Where small parts had to be made in quantity, toolmakers were required.

Body framing was made of wood, and the body builders had to be expert carpenters, working woods of different kinds and making proper mortised joints able to withstand flexing. The panellers had to be able to work plywood (a First World War invention),

thin mahogany, or sheet metal. The trimmers had to be accomplished at leather and upholstery work, and the painters at getting a smooth, durable finish over an indifferent basis, prepared by hand work alone, for such things as the power buff had yet to be invented. Bigger firms had spray painting equipment and drying ovens, but small enterprises in the early 1920s had no such equipment, and many cars were still brush-finished, a tedious business requiring many coats and much 'rubbing down' in between. There was no quick-drying cellulose to speed the process until du Pont introduced their Duco process in the USA in 1924.

It all took many more hours than it would today, and the weekly output of cars was much lower. On the other hand, demand was lower too, and by such dated methods many independent manufacturers 'got by', producing cars of fair quality for the time, and earning a living for themselves and their employees.

Henry's way

More ambitious makers could not be content with methods little changed from pre-war days. They saw the way to more profits was to build more cars at less cost by more mechanised methods, the philosophy practised so competently by Henry Ford, General Motors and other large American manufacturers. The 'mass production' so despised in the 1920s by the lay Briton and the 'quality snob' was actually practised to a small degree by any car manufacturer who made identical parts in batches. It was logical engineering, and the Americans just took it a lot further. More mechanisation meant less waste of manpower and

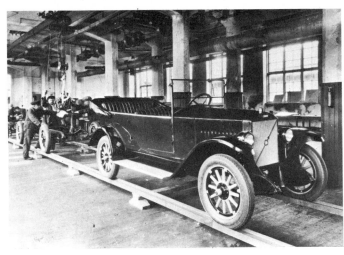

On the production line. Above *Volvo's earliest model, the American-style 2 litre four-cylinder PV4, under construction at Hisingen, Sweden, in 1927; 164 were built for the home market in two years, but Volvo cars were scarcely known abroad until after the Second World War.*

Below: *Austin six-cylinder Sixteens coming along the line in 1930 at the vast Longbridge works in Birmingham. The chassis are drawn along the assembly rails by endless ratchet chains at regular time intervals.*

closer accuracy in manufacture, since all parts were identical and therefore interchangeable, eliminating the need for individual hand fitting. Larger and more elaborate jigs and fixtures, and more of them, were used. Where the small man might fabricate small parts on the bench, the big man would prescribe a casting or pressing. Capital resources made a vital difference; where the small man could not risk ordering, say, more than 200 sets of wheels and tyres, or mudguard pressings or what-have-you, at a time, the bigger man would order 20,000 – and at a much cheaper price because of the quantity.

His production line would be properly organised, with components flowing to the assemblers in co-ordinated rhythm, while the line itself would be actuated by ratchet chains drawing the growing car along at a rate calculated precisely to allow the men to achieve their task on one car, and then to repeat it in precisely the same cycle of operations on the next car. With mass production the time phase was crucial, and the 'time and motion' experts with their stop-watches and notebooks were a regular if unpopular feature of any big factory, checking exactly how long it took to do a certain job. With all data collated, an average time would be allowed for each job, and all the countless operations in assembling a car would be co-ordinated with ruthless precision.

The unforgettable Model T Ford endured several
nicknames such as Tin Lizzie, Flivver, Jalopy, Jitney Bus
and just Henry, but its intrusion into American life
practically wrought a social revolution by bringing
motoring to the ordinary people. Here are two typical
Vintage Ts, a left-hand-drive four-door tourer of 1924
(above) finished in the black alleged to be the only colour
offered for many years. A five-seater right-hand-drive
Tudor saloon of 1927, (right) the last year of the T, when
America's most basic transport boasted bumpers,
sidelights, wire wheels etc. The car's 19-year production
span from 1908 to 1927 has been surpassed only by those
of the Rolls-Royce Silver Ghost (1907–1927) and the
VW Beetle (1945 to date).

The saving of seconds expended in needless motions became an exact science, and if to many it seemed inhuman, the object of the exercise was to build more cars more quickly at less cost. By careful study Ford cut chassis assembly time at his Highland Park factory from $12\frac{1}{2}$ to under five hours, engine assembly from nearly ten to under six hours, and flywheel magneto assembly from 20 minutes to five. "Saving a cent per part saves $12,000 a year at our rate of production" he said, and that made common sense. One of the countless Ford stories tells of the man fitting part 463 on the moving assembly line who was fired. "He dropped his monkey wrench, and while picking it up nine chassis went by." But as Henry Ford said, "Anyone who does not like to work in our way may always leave." He never went short of labour.

The fact was that in those days life was more uncertain, and the short, sharp slump had caused considerable hardship among workmen in the USA as well as in Europe. Fear of unemployment had a strong disciplinary effect, and strikes occurred only in cases of genuine grievance or hardship. Ford did not exploit his workmen; he paid the highest wages in the American motor industry, but he expected, and got, the maximum of work out of his employees during their eight hour day.

What Henry Ford did so successfully in the United States, André Citroen essayed in France, also with considerable success. In 1919 he instituted mass production methods, and one of his most successful models of the Vintage era was the almost indestructible 856cc 5CV, seen above in famous 'Cloverlead' form with central third seat in the pointed tail. Citroen introduced mass production of all-steel saloon bodies to Europe in 1925. Below: 12hp models on the assembly lines at the vast Quai Javel factory in Paris. By 1929 Citroen output was up to 100,000 vehicles per year.

Chief opposition to Citroen in France came from Renault, who produced the 8·3hp four-cylinder 6CV in reply to the Citroen 5CV. Here 'Mam'selle' in delightful vintage hat and coat demonstrates the ease with which one checks the oil dipstick on the 1926 6CV NN Weymann saloon, which has Renault's famous alligator bonnet.

The Citroen story

Naturally Ford soon had his imitators in Europe. André Citroen was a talented Dutch Jew who ran the Mors factory in Paris until he and the Hinstin brothers established a factory for making double helical (or 'chevron') gears in 1913. In the War Citroen switched to making shells of all sizes for the Allied artillery, and learnt a great deal about quantity production. In 1919 he set up as a car manufacturer, acquiring 30 acres of kitchen garden at the Quai Javel in Paris, and there erecting a factory planned from the very start for mass output.

He had brought the production of shells down to a fine art, and now wanted to do the same with cars. But he did not adopt Ford's unyielding 'one model' policy, for conditions in France did not warrant it. At first he aimed at both luxury and utilitarian markets, having prototypes made both of a $3\frac{1}{2}$ litre Knight sleeve-valve engined 'grand routier' and an economy $1\frac{1}{2}$ litre 10hp tourer of simple, robust design. When the $1\frac{1}{2}$ litre was announced in the spring of 1919 to sell at the fantastically low price of 7,500 francs, the response was so overwhelming that André Citroen unhesitatingly passed the big sleeve valve design on to Gabriel Voisin, and concentrated on the cheaper one.

This became the Type A, a rugged, unlovely work-horse of a car with 65×100mm, four-cylinder, monobloc side-valve engine and four-seater 'torpedo' (open tourer) body. It was sold complete with tyres, electric starter and lighting, items often listed as extras on apparently cheap cars. Of course the price tag of 7,500F – a quarter the 1914 figure for an equivalent model – soon rose to 7,950F, then to 12,500F, but Citroen could never build enough. He aimed at an output of 100 cars per day, but cars were proving much more complicated than shells, and he had many difficulties before getting production at the Quai Javel really under way.

Every item of the Type A was made on an assembly line, down to the wood framing and sheet metal panelling for the bodies, the running boards and the hoods, while France's first 'dip' painting was introduced for the mudguards. Output of the A was 10,000 in 1921, when it was joined by an improved B2, and a year later came the famous 5CV two-seater, finished Ford-like in one stock colour, a cheery lemon yellow inviting the sobriquet 'Citron', and with a distinctive

turned-up pointed tail. A year after that a dickey seat was let into the tail, and the famous 'Cloverleaf' Citroen was born. Terribly erect two-seater cabriolet and four-seater saloon Citroens followed, but there was common-sense in straight edges which could more easily be made than curves when turning out thousands and thousands.

Citroen output in 1923 was up to 150 cars per day, and over 250 per day by 1925, when Citroen became the first European manufacturer to mass-produce all-steel bodies (under US licence). By 1926 Citroen had absorbed both Clément-Bayard and his old firm, Mors, and the cars with the double-chevron trade mark were being assembled in England, Belgium, Germany, Austria and Italy as well as in the much enlarged Quai Javel plant. Balloon tyres, Westinghouse servo brakes, cellulose finish (the first in Europe) and more shapely, rounded steel bodies added to their attractions, and by 1928 Citroen were building 36 per cent of France's car production. With his name in lights on the Eiffel Tower by then, André Citroen seemed to have reached the summit, and forged on a wave of success into the troubled 1930s.

Other mass producers

Of other French manufacturers, Renault, Mathis and Peugeot, had adopted mass production to varying degrees, as had Opel in Germany and Fiat in Italy. Renault's products still retained their scuttle radiators and 'alligator' bonnets of prewar days, Mathis built ugly small cars with four-speed gearboxes, and Peugeot, like Renault, built a wide range of cars. Opel suffered like all German concerns in the immediate post-war years, and built more bicycles than cars until, in 1924, they installed American-type conveyor belt assembly lines and began to build a Teutonic copy of the Citroen 5CV. It had one standard colour, green, and it was dubbed the *Laubfrosch* or tree toad. Opel built many thousands of them, supplemented by

other worthy but dull motor cars, and were absorbed by the American General Motors Corporation in 1929.

Fiat of Italy manufactured many excellent, tough, lively cars from 1919, the 1½ litre side-valve 501 being the staple product, with sporting variants. Britain's great apostle of mass, or 'quantity' production as it was carefully called, was, of course, William Morris with his highly successful Oxford and Cowley models which went from strength to strength in the 1920s, largely combatting the Ford hold on the market. But other makers also took what was an inevitable road, if not so wholeheartedly as Morris, and increased their output through 'quantity' production. Austin of Longbridge was one, Bean, Clyno, Standard and Singer were among others.

The Clyno story is a particularly harrowing one. Based in Wolverhampton, they switched from making high-quality motorcycles to cars in 1922. Their first four-wheeler typified the car built largely from proprietary parts (though they made their own gearboxes) and the permutation proved a happy one, for the 10·8 Clyno was lively, steered and braked well and, most important, was reliable and economical. It became highly popular as an alternative to the eternal Morris Cowley, and by 1927 Clyno was offering a four-wheel braked four-door saloon at little more than the price of a two-door Cowley.

But it was all a great strain for an under-sized, under-capitalised company, and the beginning of the end came when a Clyno Nine two-door fabric saloon was introduced at a price of £160. On a mere rumour that Morris was working on a £100 car they broke themselves trying to cheapen their excellent new Nine. They gave it an open body with primitive hood and minimal lighting equipment, and called it the Clyno Century, although they could not get the price below £112 10s. Coupled with a lapse in quality and performance standards on their other models,

Vintage bread-and-butter.
Left: *the American line shows itself in the Citroen C4 of 1928, a sturdy, all-steel 1·5 litre saloon; a six-cylinder version, the C6, was also marketed.*
Above: *although seen here surprisingly taking part in a German touring car race, the 951cc Opel 4/12PS represented transport at its most basic. It was a close copy of the 5CV Citroen.*

Below: *one of Britain's best-known Vintage makes was the Clyno, which rivalled the Morris Cowley in providing sound, cheap transport with good handling and four wheel brakes. This is a 1927 10·8 'Royal' tourer, with one of the first motorists' caravans, a 1924 Eccles, in tow.*

Clyno's good reputation was tainted and sales wavered, then fell with the start of the Depression. On top of it all, they had an ambitious new factory to pay for. By March 1929 it was all up for Clyno and the receivers were in.

The £100 lure

The £100 car was a will o' the wisp pursued by others in the vintage era. Carden tried it with their cycle-car in 1920, but it was not so easy to build a proper small car to such a price. The little-known Gillett concern tried in 1926 with a neat open two-seater having an advanced four-cylinder overhead valve engine, three-speed gearbox and four-wheel brakes. The rear axle had no differential – always an early casualty when costs have to be cut – and springing

Despite this bold 1926 proclamation, the 10hp Seaton-Petter £100 car with vertical twin two-stroke engine had disappeared a year later. It took three further years and all the resources of Morris Motors Ltd. to produce a true £100 car, the side-valve Minor (below), and then it was only a two-seater with austere equipment, black-painted radiator and headlamps, and no sidelights.

was by quarter-elliptics all round. It was an early user of rack-and-pinion steering when that excellent system was looked down on as 'dangerous', but the public scarcely sampled it. The British Ensign Co. of Willesden, makers of a large, poorly selling luxury car, were to build the Gillett, but at a time when the cheapest rival small car cost £145 someone's costing must have been optimistic, for only 25 Gilletts were ever made.

The Waverley concern, also of Willesden, also essayed a £100 car, theirs having a 900cc rear-mounted water-cooled flat-twin engine and friction driven through four speeds. It did not go into production, while the Seaton-Petter project from Yeovil was also stillborn. This one had a 1·3 litre two-stroke twin-cylinder engine, three speeds, and a large open four-seater body which also served as a truck by removing the rear seats. Not until the very end of the vintage era, at the close of 1930, was a £100 car – a very basic Morris Minor two-seater – actually marketed, and even this one did not survive long without a price increase.

Yet on the other side of the Atlantic the USA had long had an equivalent of an under £100 car in the Ford Model T, which as the 1920s advanced continued to pour off the lines. Its price dropped as production rose, from $355 in 1920 when 1,250,000 were built, to $295 in 1923 – a figure which, with dollar value at circa five shillings (25p) to the £ meant approximately £74! Production peaked that year at 2,055,309! In Britain the Manchester-assembled T cost over twice as much at £165, yet was a bargain at that despite the unfavourable RAC horsepower tax.

By 1926 the T cost only $290, but despite more attractive bodywork the magic was fading. Rivals such as Chevrolet, the 'cheap arm' of General Motors, were thrusting in with more modern cars, and T sales began to tail off. The Gray, a rival Detroiter built by ex-Ford employees, challenged but died after four

FERGUSON.

years, but the Durant made inroads, as did the Overland, a stern rival ever since 1914, and one doing very well in export markets. There was also Dodge, first to mass-produce an all-steel saloon body in 1924, and the Essex, a cheaper offshoot of the Hudson. None of these could quite get down to Ford's amazing prices, but all were more modern in specification, and all found ready markets. By 1926 Model T sales were down to 1,629,184 – still a stupendous figure – and between January and May 1927 only 380,741 Ts were built, and then production of the model was halted completely.

In all 15,007,133 Model T Fords were manufactured between 1908 and 1927, an output only surpassed by another model, the Volkswagen 'Beetle', in 1972. The shutdown lasted over six months, during which Ford retooled and changed production lines over to the new Model A. Those expecting another Ford miracle expressed themselves disappointed at this very ordinary successor to the T. It had a beefy 3·3 litre four cylinder side-valve engine, an orthodox three-speed gearbox in place of the T's epicyclic two-speed, four wheel brakes and wire wheels with notably thick spokes. But Henry Ford had not lost his grip, and the

Above: ease of access emphasised on a 1927 12hp Swift coachbuilt saloon. Note typical vintage features such as the roof-peak, running board carrying the battery, Sankey artillery wheels and externally-mounted spare wheel.
Below: the car that set the British standard for price and dependability, the 11·9 'Bullnose' Morris Cowley. This example is a 1925 six-light saloon with no offside doors, and running board laden with spare 2-gallon petrol can, toolbox and spare wheel.

Economy small car by Rover, the Eight of 1920–25, had a transverse air-cooled flat-twin side-valve engine of 998cc (later 1130cc) and refined shaft and worm gear final-drive elevating it from the cyclecar class. About 17000 of these simple, sturdy vehicles were built.

And by Morris. . . . The Minor introduced in 1929 was a neat but uncomfortably compact four-seater fabric-bodied saloon, powered by a lively little four-cylinder 847cc water-cooled engine with an overhead camshaft. Priced at £125 it proved a stern rival to the Austin Seven.

A matched its greatest rival, Chevrolet, 4½ million being built between 1928 and 1932, and that despite the great world depression of 1929–1931.

The big depression

In 1929 American automobile production reached a new peak of 4,794,898 cars built – 85 per cent of the world's cars were manufactured by American-owned companies, which makes the efforts of Morris, Renault, Citroen, Opel, Fiat and other major Europeans seem very modest. Then, in late October, came the Wall Street crash and the world financial crisis. The bottom fell out of business, US car output in 1930 dropped to 2,910,187, and the decade ended with the automobile industry up against it, the major American makes largely living on the accumulated fat of the boom years, the smaller ones perceptibly weakening. Several went to the wall as the depression lingered on into the 1930s.

Shock waves from the stock market collapse in New York spread across the Atlantic to Europe in the next few months, hitting the motor industry harder than many, since the car still constituted a luxury rather than a necessity. The result was death to many fine luxury-class large cars, and a swing by essential motorists to small, cheap, economical ones – and that meant more mass production and fewer quality hand-made cars.

In Britain the Austin Seven had already been joined in 1928 by the Clyno Century, the Standard Nine with worm final drive, the Triumph Super Seven with four-wheel hydraulic brakes, and the Morris Minor with a four-cylinder engine having an overhead camshaft inherited via Wolseley (whom Morris had taken over) from the Hispano-Suiza aero-engine of the First World War.

As such models firmly entrenched themselves on the market, the true vintage car with its individuality and meticulous construction died, for manufacturers fighting a war for survival against costs could not indulge in the luxury of skilled craftsmen when cheaper labour could build cheaper cars with soulless precision by extensive mechanisation. Firms that struggled to maintain design quality by the old methods dropped from the tree one by one, only a few surviving by sheer character to better times. Thus the decade which opened in such a frenzy of extravagant buying closed in a chastened mood of austerity. Yet the best of its products between these extremes lived on far beyond it as monuments to a creative era.

THE NEW MOTORING

'... motoring is always so fresh, so surprising, and so young-
in-manner a pastime that the quite old as well as the quite
young are carried away by its radiated delights, and
constantly the middle-aged say, as it were, to
themselves, "This is a splendid pastime, what
did we do in the old days without it?"'

The Autocar, December 28, 1923

Forty or fifty years ago roads were very different to those of today. There was not the overwhelming volume of traffic, nor the bustle, noise and fumes that go with it. I lived when a boy in a typical suburban area outside London, at Sunbury-on-Thames, and as mad-keen motor enthusiasts from the age of seven I well remember my elder brother and myself eagerly scanning the village street for the next car to come along.

More often than not it was a 'Bullnose' Morris Cowley (I can still hear the curiously high exhaust note and squealing brakes), but among other regulars in the district we came to recognise was an Angus Sanderson tourer used by the local electrician, a Calcott with a radiator like a Standard, a Standard with a radiator like a Calcott, a Clyno or two, an ugly black Hands, a Rhode which, its proud owner insisted right up to 1932, 'had a racing engine' because it had an overhead camshaft and aluminium pistons, and the two station taxis, a Unic on the south side and a Renault two-cylinder on the north. This meant it had frequently to climb the railway bridge, which, so its driver insisted, it tackled with brave "I think I can, I think I can, I thiiiink I caaaan" noises from its engine, diminishing anxiously as it neared the crest, then thankfully accelerating again to "I knew I could, I knew I could, I knew I could . . ." as it clattered downhill.

One car in five minutes was considered 'busy', and we had to walk a mile to Sunbury Cross or the Staines Road to see more. Kempton Park on a race day was paradise, bringing a host of extra cars which were often re-routed through our road to avoid con-

gestion(!), and one could scarcely take in the stream of chauffeur-driven Daimlers, Rolls-Royces, Sunbeams, Packards and lesser makes – Armstrong-Siddeleys with those unpleasant disc wheels, American cars that all looked the same apart from clattering Model T Fords, and the inevitable Morrises and Austins, all moving so slowly that we could read the names on the radiators and move on to the next. We had no eye for the occupants, just the cars, and once I saw a rich, plum-coloured, and to me old-fashioned looking Daimler, and was told in awe-stricken tones by a neighbour that it contained Queen Mary.

The accursed kerbstone which delineates every road today marked only major highways in those

Epsom downs in Derby week, 1920, with a variety of old and new means of transport. The centre car is a Lagonda.

39

The ubiquitous motor car. . . .
Above: *the City of London in the rain, circa 1926, with a Clyno, a Standard and a Daimler recognisable on a slippery-looking wood block road – but without the prohibitive white or yellow lines of today, or attendant wardens.*

Below: *Rio de Janeiro in the sun, circa 1923, with American cars dominating – and every one a tourer in testimony to the South American climate.*

days. For the rest, the roads were edged by natural grass verges. Lamp posts went as far as the houses and no farther, and were lit by gas, with a little blue by-pass light and time clock if 'modern', or more often a chain for the lamp lighter to pull down with his special pole. Traffic 'instruction' for school children amounted to the usual advice about 'looking both ways' and 'let the policeman take you across', and a list of "Danger Don'ts" on the back of our exercise books, advising us, among other things, not to play 'Last across' on a busy street, and not to startle the milkman's horse.

There were no traffic lights, no one-way streets, no yellow lines, no zebra or Belisha pedestrian crossings nor crossing wardens; just the village policeman at the busiest junction during the 'busy' time when the toilers streamed to work or home from the village's one big factory, mostly on bicycles, some on foot, and only 'the bosses' in cars. There were no specific bus stops then; you just hailed and the General double-decker bus, an AEC K-type on 'our' route, would stop, its solid tyres pounding hard on the tarred road. Cows left their trail on the road, plodding from the farm on one side to the meadow a half-mile further up on the other side, and nobody worried. By-roads were not metalled at all, but had a sandy top surface which filled with puddles when it rained. Busier places such as Hampton Court had shiny tramlines and rough, greasy cobbles.

The vintage garage

Our local garage had a Shell hand-operated petrol pump, with a globe atop a long neck, a sight glass to show the petrol flowing, and a white price panel which probably said "1s 3d per gal." or thereabouts. Inside was a stack of two-gallon cans of petrol, for motorists still had the habit of carrying some reserve fixed on the running board; there was also an aged and dusty limousine of unknown make lurking in a corner, a black-faced minion in greasy overalls who periodically came up for air from within car bonnets, a forge, a pedal-operated grinder ('come on, son, lend us your foot'), a grease-filled cobblestone floor, sundry chipped and veined enamel signs saying 'Sternol', 'John Bull Tyres' and 'Gabriel Snubbers' (which quite baffled me – I thought it was a person!) and a smug new, shiny sign saying 'You may telephone from here'.

The owner ran a curious Morris Cowley two-seater with a box at the back instead of a dickey seat – a special commercial traveller's model, apparently, while stuck out in the yard in all weathers was an old WD Crossley with a low brass radiator, big wire wheels and thin tyres, duplicated at the rear, and a crane on the back for hauling in breakdowns.

Of course all roads were infinitely less busy in the 1920s. In Britain the motor industry produced 132,000 private cars in 1925, compared with 1,742,000 in 1971! Around Sunbury way there were perhaps fewer cars than gravel lorries – solid-tyred, ex-service Leylands, AECs and Peerlesses, and Sentinel steam wagons, which thudded along all day, leaving a long, wet sandy trail behind them, and contribut-

Every mod con. . . .
Above: *a Surrey picnic scene, 1922, with the wireless picking up 2LO, aided by that lofty clamp-on aerial, Junior all agog with earphones on, and the kettle boiling on the spirit stove.*

Below: *plenty of space to pull up on either side of the way and examine the Sailor's Grave on the Portsmouth Road. The boat-tailed two-seater is a special-bodied Morris.*
Below, right: *gathering for a point-to-point in about 1922, with a three-wheeler 'runabout' and a Crossley tourer prominent.*

ing, no doubt, to the many potholes in the district. The average road was narrow and pleasantly winding, but schemes were afoot for modernising all the major trunk roads, and not many miles from us a fantastic new 'super-road' called the Kingston bypass was being built.

There was an outdated general speed limit of 20mph, which apparently most drivers generously interpreted as nearer 30mph while keeping an eye alert for a police helmet. Car taxation at 2 guineas for up to 6½ horsepower, 3 guineas for 6½ to 12 horsepower, 4 guineas for 12 to 16 horsepower, etc., and a driving licence costing 5 shillings, were the sole re-

One parked free of care in vintage motoring days. A Singer 10 in Reigate, Surrey, in 1924.

quisites to go motoring. One had to be at least 17 years of age, there was no driving test to pass, and one merely applied for the licence to one's county council. Insurance was an option, not obligatory, but if you kept a chauffeur you had to pay 15 shillings per annum for a licence "to keep a male servant", while use of armorial bearings or heraldic devices was taxed at two guineas per year. . . .

Roads abroad

Conditions were much the same in other countries, spiced by local characteristics. The better French roads, such as the Routes Nationales, were splendidly straight and fast, delineated by the familiar rows of poplar trees on both sides. Neglect through the War and the difficult years just after it had left them rather rough and pot-holed until the mid-1920s, while those in the battle areas remained in a deplorable condition for many years.

Belgium's roads suffered abominably through the First World War, while their *pavé* surfaces never were very sympathetic to motor cars. Italy's road system, after stagnating for many years, had a shot in the arm with the advent of Mussolini's Fascist government, which inaugurated vigorous reconstruction and built Europe's first motorways, known as *autostrade*, beginning in 1924 with a 30-mile stretch from Milan to Varese. In Germany the Government had announced an *autostrasse* programme as early as 1923, and only economic difficulties prevented its realisation before the advent of Hitler and his *autobahnen* of the late 1930s.

In the United States, where a much larger population of automobiles (registrations between 1919 and 1930 rose from a staggering 6,679 million to a stupefying 22,972 million!) was scattered over a much larger area, road development just had to be pushed forward. Surprisingly, roads in some of the more rural states were little more than dirt or mud tracks, but many thousands of miles of road were laid or improved, asphalt or concrete replacing gravel, cobbles and the sinister gumbo, but as fast as they were completed the teeming automobiles seemed to catch up and fill them. With so many cars, town centres which

grew up around horse-drawn traffic proved totally inadequate, and America was encountering parking problems in the vintage era which we in Europe did not experience until thirty years later.

In general, whatever the country, the roads were narrower, more scenic, less ordered and disciplined than now, but pleasantly free and offering the magic of the skyline and beyond to the new motorists of the vintage era. In America the car was already an essential adjunct to family life, but in Europe despite the great post-war upsurge of interest, it was still too expensive for everyone to indulge, and traffic stayed tolerably spread out. To many in Britain, motoring was still a seasonal occupation, and the spring bank holidays would bring the first jams of cars newly taxed for the warm weather period.

The middle makes

What sort of cars would one encounter in these early jams, so mild and rare compared with the maddening modern rush-hour build-up that occurs each day in most towns? Invariably there was class distinction among cars, as with people. Of the modest cyclecars and smaller cars we have already said something in earlier chapters, while later in this book we shall review the cars for the rich. Between these two categories came a middle-price class echelon, represented in Britain by such worthy makes as AC, Crossley, Humber, Talbot, Wolseley, the larger Rovers, and several other makes now expired, such as Vulcan, Arrol-Johnston and Star.

The AC (the initials stand for Auto-Carriers, founded long before the First World War) had an advanced 2 litre six-cylinder engine with cast aluminium block and a single chain-driven overhead camshaft. Designed by Weller, this fine unit was used in the same basic form from 1919 to 1965, an extraordinary record of longevity. In its vintage phase its virtues were somewhat offset by use of an inadequate three-speed gearbox mounted on the rear axle, and incorporating a disc brake. Even so, the AC had a good reputation for quality and also for performance, supported by many long distance class records and the first British victory in the Monte Carlo Rally, in 1926.

Manchester's Crossley was a long-established make, rather old-fashioned in design but extremely well built, which gained a splendid reputation in the First World War with its ambulances, trucks and staff-cars. A popular post-war model was the rugged 14hp with 2·4 litre side-valve four-cylinder engine, three-speed gearbox, and underslung rear springs. There was also the larger 19·6 with 3·8 litre engine, and a sports variant. All Crossleys epitomised the craftsman-built British car, sound, solid and dependable, and to such a traditional firm 'mass production' was anathema, and when the pace became too much for them in the 1930s they withdrew and concentrated on lorry and bus manufacture.

Humber of Coventry, pioneer cycle makers, enjoyed a similar reputation to Crossley with a sound, conventional range of family cars. Rover, too, had

All sorts and sizes made up the Vintage scene.
Top: *a 1925 Talbot 10/23 with 1100cc pushrod overhead valve engine, one of Britain's best small cars.* Above: *the very American looking Fiat 521C coupe of 1929. It had a 2·5 litre six-cylinder side-valve power unit.*

Top: *a 1926 six-cylinder example of that much respected French marque, Delaunay-Belleville.* Above: *a rare one from Sweden, the 4·4 litre four-cylinder Scania-Vabis Type F4A Phaeton, a model first built in 1912 by a concern famous today for its heavy trucks.* Below: *a 1925 Weymann-bodied 26·9hp Renault.*

Quality from Wolverhampton: a 1926 Star 14/40 two-seater with 2 litre ohv four-cylinder engine.

Enterprise from Detroit: a 1926 Chrysler 60 two-seater with hydraulically operated external contracting brakes.

begun with bicycles, and beside the small, noisy but economical air-cooled flat-twin 8 they built the four-cylinder side valve '12' and in 1925 introduced larger fours with overhead camshafts and hemispherical combustion chambers. The Talbot of the 1920s was an excellent design by the Swiss Georges Roesch, who produced the lively 10/23 based on the 8/18, both with flexible four-cylinder overhead-valve engines, and the 12/30, later 14/45, with six cylinders and outstanding performance.

Wolseley, a Birmingham marque founded in 1895 with Herbert (later Lord) Austin as designer, belonged to Vickers Ltd after the First World War, and built a quality Ten and a 15, both with overhead camshaft engines inspired by the Hispano-Suiza V8 aero-engine which Wolseley had built in quantity during the war. By 1925 these models were enlarged, and a new overhead camshaft six was introduced shortly before the Company went bankrupt. There was an American bid to take the concern over, but Sir William Morris got in first, and Wolseley became part of his growing empire in 1927.

Vulcan were based at Southport, and were better known for their commercial vehicles. Their cars were somewhat conservative and usually used Dorman engines, although from 1923 they had a liaison with Lea-Francis of Coventry, the two makes pooling manufacture of various parts. It availed them little, and the last Vulcan car was built in 1928, a year after the last Arrol-Johnston. This famous Scottish make was in at the birth of the British automobile industry, and was notable for trying out four wheel brakes as early as 1909. A much publicised 'Victory' model with a 2·6 litre overhead camshaft engine flopped badly in 1919–1920, but older designs such as the 15·9, the 14 and 20hp four-cylinder models sustained the firm until its demise following a combine with the Aster concern of Wembley, Middlesex, and the adoption of sleeve valve engines.

Star was a Wolverhampton firm who built good looking, quality fours and sixes, adopting overhead valves and four wheel brakes in 1926. However, Star went bankrupt in 1932.

Why did these manufacturers (and they were by no means the only ones), who took pride in their workmanship, suffer the ignominy of bankruptcy? Theirs was the unhappy fate of many ageing concerns in many countries, which did not adjust to changing conditions, and failed to re-equip their factories for modern methods of production, either through lack of foresight, or of capital, or sheer dislike of the new system. Although surviving examples of such makes now epitomise the better class of vintage car, at the time they could not compete on price with go-ahead quantity-production makes such as Austin and Morris, and one by one fell by the wayside.

France had her middle class too – the Delaunay-Belleville, Delahaye and Darracq, and Ballot, the new marque introduced by the former proprietary engine makers, and Hotchkiss, most of whose cars were characterised by rather sombre close-coupled Weymann-type bodies, a popular patent constructional system employing flexibly jointed wood framing with leather or fabric covering.

Italy had the larger Fiats such as the six-cylinder 510, the Itala, and the advanced Lancia Lambda which had integral chassis/body construction and independent front suspension by vertical coil springs in 1922.

Germany, emerging through chaos to brief stability by 1924–25, had a surprising number of medium price makes. In addition to the smaller Mercedes,

Elegance from Indianapolis, exemplified by the Cole Aero-Eight of 1923, which had a 5·4 litre V8 power unit.

The CHEVROLET *Eight*

$1385.00

f.o.b. Flint

If you saw a Chevrolet eight cylinder, five passenger touring car for the first time and did not know the price of it, you would be apt to estimate it at a figure far above the actual purchasing amount.

In detail, in distinguished appearance, this model has every mark of the thoroughbred car.

The body is a delight to the eye. Not an angle anywhere—only a series of curves that blend harmoniously. There is grace in its poise—a richness in its finish—which is highly distinctive. And the body has more than looks—it has comfort, easy riding qualities, and unusual spring suspension.

Quality materials of guaranteed excellence are used in its construction throughout.

All visible woodwork is of genuine mahogany; and all metal parts from door locks to steering post and windshield are of bright nickel. The invisible foundation of the body is built of pressed steel.

Elegant upholstering of French-pleated leather surrounds the extra deep seats, wide backs, and spacious door pockets. You ride here in ease, in extreme comfort, with a feeling of complete relaxation. And you feel proud of the finish—a rich, lustrous Chevrolet green, artfully applied by hand.

Vintage advertising by Chevrolet (above) over-exploits the old technique of small people in a big car; the driver of this V8 could never, surely, reach the pedals.

Below: heavy retouching suggests that Erskine of Indiana seated occupants behind a plywood facsimile of their 1927 2·3 litre touring six for this publicity photograph.

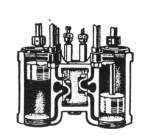

Despite the optimism of this advertisement, Stanley steam car production ended in 1926, outmoded and outpriced by petrol. Right: a 1925 Doble, most sophisticated of all steamers, its engine giving 119bhp at a velvet 940rpm – and no gears to change. The flash boiler supplied superheated steam in 40–45 secs, but the Doble was virtually dead by 1927.

there were Stoewer, Simson, Protos, NSU, Adler, Dux and Benz, all of them building sound, solid Teutonic cars, with the German, Austrian, Czech, Polish and Scandinavian markets to absorb them.

In the vast United States market, intermediate-price manufacturers were legion. General Motors alone controlled Buick, Oldsmobile and Oakland, which became Pontiac in 1926, while independents included Dodge, Hudson, Nash, Hupmobile and the Maxwell, product of an ailing concern which was taken over by 'trouble shooter' Walter Chrysler in 1922. The Maxwell gave way in 1924 to the advanced Chrysler 70 with high compression six-cylinder, seven-bearing engine and four wheel hydraulic external contracting brakes. The Chrysler Corporation subsequently took over Dodge, then launched two new challengers to Chevrolet, the Plymouth four and the de Soto six.

In general American cars were monotonously similar with their wood-spoked wheels, combined wings and running boards, their fashions such as drum-shaped headlights, and two or four door sedan bodies. But the cars were well engineered, and with their large, lightly stressed engines, were reliable and long-lasting, a heavy fuel consumption being no great worry in a country where 'gas' was extremely cheap in comparison with European prices.

The end of steam

The sheer efficiency attained by conventional American cars by the middle 1920s sounded the death knell of the steam car. This form of power, at

its best simple, silent, flexible and cheap, still has its staunch adherents today, seeking a way round the steamer's shortcomings. Among these were the time taken 'firing up' from cold (i.e., for the heater to turn the water into steam); the acrid smell of the kerosene used in many burners; boiler deposits from hard water and lubricants; the weight of the components and their cost.

Mechanically the steam car of the early 1920s, epitomised by the famous Stanley, had scarcely changed since before the war, yet the 1923 model cost over $800 against the Model T Ford's $295, and when in good mechanical condition the Ford had the advantages of quick mobility from cold, and consistent engine performance. Maintaining consistent pressure on the Stanley was always a problem; initial acceleration and hillclimbing were phenomenal, but as steam was consumed and more water admitted, performance dropped off.

The steam car also had its own complex system of controls, whereas the petrol car layout had become standardised with three pedals, gear and brake levers, and manual ignition control. Despite its smooth, silent performance, the lack of irksome gears and clutch, and the charm of drawing your motive power free from a stream or river, the steam car steadily lost ground to petrol. Stanley, the only builder of steamers in appreciable quantities by then, gave up the fight in 1925, but Abner Doble persevered with his large, imposing, complicated and expensive creations for a few years more.

Had more manufacturers taken an interest in the steam car, they could well have perfected its functioning to that pitch enjoyed by the internal combustion engine, which was achieved thanks only to years and years of development. As it was, petrol had too many advantages in the 1920s. Yet – who knows? – future pollution laws, or a world shortage of petroleum, could force major attention back to steam as a motive power some day.

CARS FOR THE RICH

'Throughout automobile history, three names have been outstanding: Rolls-Royce, Hispano-Suiza, and Isotta-Fraschini. One is English, one Spanish, and one Italian. Of the three, two have disappeared. Only the British product has remained, imperturbable, unchanged and unchallenged for 40 to 50 years. This is a rare phenomenon...'

Motori Torino, **1962**

Cost was ever the tyrant in car design, and the designer given *carte blanche* to produce the finest motor carriage possible, with no reservations about price, size, ease of production, or fuel consumption, should have been a happy man. In the exhilaration of the early 1920s, almost every motor manufacturing country, not excluding Spain and Czechoslovakia, essayed to produce the ultimate in automobiles, even if some had second thoughts about putting them into production. The finest and rarest fruits of vintage engineering are to be found in this fascinating 'Croesus' class, and by their near-perfection and longevity have unwittingly contributed to the legend that *all* vintage cars were good.

Because it has been so consistently successful, it is customary to genuflect before Rolls-Royce as the epitome of craftsmanship, quality, refinement and elegance in cars. Certainly the British marque has had a longer run in the uppermost echelon than any other, right from 1907 and the first 40/50 six-cylinder car to the present day, and none can deny the superlative excellence of the best Rolls-Royce designs such as the Silver Ghost, the Phantoms, and later models. Rival designer Laurence H. Pomeroy Senr. rather cruelly called the Rolls-Royce "a triumph of workmanship over design", and indeed the manufacturing standards imposed by the perfectionist Sir Henry Royce guaranteed the finest possible production around proven principles rather than resort to the latest design practices.

The vintage Rolls-Royce 40/50 Silver Ghost had basically the same 7·4 litre six-cylinder, twelve-plug, seven-bearing side-valve engine used in the pre-war model, but equipped with aluminium pistons and driving through a separate four-speed gearbox. The chassis had semi-elliptic front springs, cantilever rear springs, two very effective rear brakes up to 1923, and four-wheel brakes with Hispano-Suiza-type mechanical servo from 1924. Needless to say, everything was made to Royce's exacting standards, with rigorous inspection throughout to justify the proud claim "The Best Car in the World".

With only the highest class coachbuilders practising their art on the 40/50 chassis, the typical vintage Silver Ghost possessed the most superbly balanced proportions, enhanced by that unique square-cut radiator which has survived regally through the years. A smaller and less impressive Rolls-Royce, the Twenty with 3·1 litre overhead valve six-cylinder engine, was introduced in 1922, while in 1925 the 18-year-old Silver Ghost was replaced by the Phantom with 7·7 litre overhead valve engine. This saw R-R most adequately to the close of the vintage era, when the still further refined Phantom II succeeded it. The Silver Ghost and Phantom I were also manufactured at an American Rolls-Royce factory at Springfield, Mass., from 1920 until 1931.

Partly, perhaps, because they too have hyphenated names and sound even more exotic, Hispano-Suiza and Isotta-Fraschini are invariably bracketed with Rolls-Royce among the elite of automobiles. Despite its Spanish-Swiss origins (the concern was founded in 1904 in Barcelona by the Spaniards Castro and Mateu, and the Swiss designer Marc Birkigt), the Hispano-Suiza was widely regarded as France's "Rolls-Royce" or top prestige car. The French branch had opened in

49

'The Best Car in the World', most challenging slogan by any manufacturer, has been copyrighted by Rolls-Royce for many years, and upheld by products of a splendour, quality and refinement difficult to equal. Glorious Vintage examples, such as the 7·7 litre 40/50 Phantom 1 aluminium tourer (opposite), and the elegant 1924 Silver Ghost (above) obscure the fact that the 40/50 six-cylinder design was distinctly Edwardian, first appearing in 1907 and enduring until 1925. Above the distinctive scuttle treatment of the white tourer, with nautical wood slatting and ventilators, and the clearly marked controls. Left and right: two examples of the smaller, less attractive Vintage Rolls-Royce, the 3·1 litre overhead valve 20hp. Preceding page: a 1925 open Silver Ghost in the Alps.

1911, and after the War they turned their unique knowledge of building over 50,000 140 bhp aluminium alloy, overhead camshaft aero engines to good account in a superb new car which far outdid the conservative Rolls-Royce on specification.

Revealed at the 1919 Paris Salon, the 6·6 litre Type H6B had an in-line six-cylinder engine in aluminium with screwed-in steel liners, a single overhead camshaft, and an output of 135 bhp. This gave such a performance that four wheel brakes were deemed essential by Birkigt, who designed them with servo-assistance through a drum driven off the three-speed gearbox. Naturally the elite of Continental *carrossiers*, such as Kellner, Saoutchik, Binder and Vanvooren rushed to clothe this superb engine and chassis with their most elegant bodywork, set off by the famous 'flying stork' radiator mascot which Birkigt adopted

in memory of French air ace Guynemer's "Stork squadron".

Italy's "Rolls-Royce" was the Isotta-Fraschini Tipo 8A, a vast car which made a sensation in 1919, for it had the world's first straight-eight engine to go into production. This was a 5·9 litre unit with nine main bearings, tubular connecting rods, pushrod overhead valves, and the mild output of 80 bhp at 2,200 rpm but impressive torque. The car had a three-speed gearbox with such wide ratios that it was often

Above: recalling past splendours, an ornate Rolls-Royce Silver Ghost and a Crossley seen during the Prince of Wales' state visit to India in 1922–23.
Below: large dimensions are fully exploited in this superb torpédo body on the 1924 32CV Hispano-Suiza chassis.

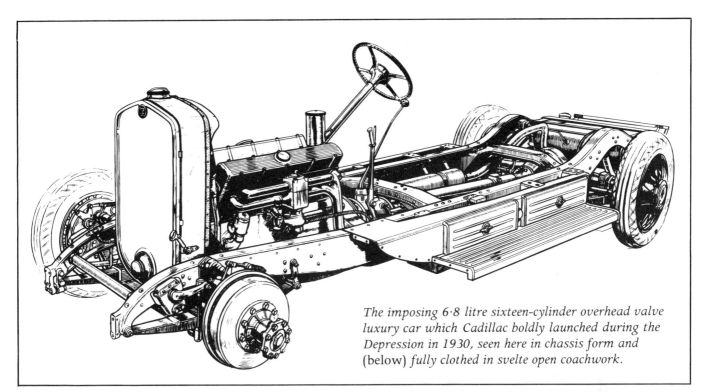

The imposing 6·8 litre sixteen-cylinder overhead valve luxury car which Cadillac boldly launched during the Depression in 1930, seen here in chassis form and (below) fully clothed in svelte open coachwork.

easier not to change down, the massive engine easily coping with top gear starts. With a 12ft 1in wheelbase, servo four-wheel brakes, and a weight of almost 3 tons the car had a maximum speed of about 80mph. In 1924 the 8B appeared, fitted with a larger 7·4 litre 120bhp engine. The cream of Italy's bodybuilders such as Cesare Sala, Farina and Castagna, and the best-known Paris houses, fitted coachwork to the cars, which had a considerable market in the United States, notably in Hollywood, until the Depression.

America's ultimates

America had her own top luxury cars in the 1920s, such as the Cadillac, Packard and Duesenberg. With deeper roots in the industry than the new Duesenberg marque, the former two both had impeccable reputations for smooth, silent, reliable carriages, and waged an interesting multi-cylinder battle for several years. In 1915 Cadillac had launched their sensational 5·1 litre V8, which set new standards in silent, efficient luxury travel. It had the electric self-starting and lighting which Cadillac had pioneered three years earlier, and but for Europe's preoccupation with the War, this V8 would have made greater international impact.

Packard countered with their "Twin-Six", the

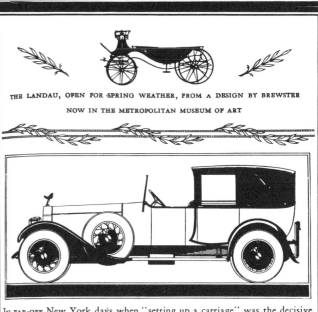

American car designers in Vintage days enjoyed the
advantages of almost limitless road miles and cheap fuel.
As a result the average American car was generous both in
chassis and engine dimensions, giving effortless
performance and a high degree of comfort. A style leader
in the 1920s was the new Chrysler marque, born in 1924,
and despite the garish and non-standard finish of the
example seen (opposite) racing at a 1972 Vintage meeting,
the six-cylinder '70' of 1929 set a fashion with its swept
wings, 'ribbon-edged' radiator and clean lines which were
widely copied.
Left: the air-cooled Franklin is a popular classic today.
The 1928 26 hp six-cylinder sedan had conservative lines
for the time, and this particular example once belonged
to famous aviator Col. Charles Lindbergh.

Above: another quality American car was the Stutz,
built at Indianapolis. This 4 litre overhead camshaft
six-cylinder Black Hawk sedan was introduced in 1929
as a less expensive line to boost sales.

world's first production V12, which was built from 1916 to 1923. Its engine measured 6·9 litres, had side valves and aluminium pistons. It was the Packard engine which first inspired Enzo Ferrari with his love for twelve-cylinder engines, but it was replaced in 1923 by a more modern 5·9 litre straight eight. Cadillac continued building their V8, with many refinements (including the world's first synchromesh gearbox in 1929), and then astonished the motoring world a second time with their new 16 cylinder car in 1930. This had its cylinders in a 45 degree vee, overhead valves, a capacity of 7·4 litres, and an output of 185 bhp. Despite the Depression it sold well for several years. Packard's reply, another super-luxury V12, followed two years later, although ironically both makes ended up by making V8s.

The Duesenberg brothers August and Frederick came to luxury car production through racing and engine manufacture for cars, boats and aircraft before and during the First World War. Their Model A private car, announced in 1920, scored two important 'firsts': it was America's first production straight-eight, and was the first to have four wheel brakes. These, moreover, were hydraulically operated by a system using glycerine and water instead of the oil which later became universal. Unlike the straight-eight Isotta-Fraschini, the American engine had only three broad main bearings; the valves were operated by a single overhead camshaft, while duralumin tubular connecting rods and Magnalite alloy pistons smacked of racing practice.

Capacity was 4·26 litres, and this fine engine turned quite fast for its time, delivering 92 bhp at 3,800 rpm. A three-speed gearbox was deemed adequate, and road weight was 3,100 lb, giving the car a maximum speed of around 85 mph with heavy coachwork. This first road Duesenberg lacked the really striking bodywork its European rivals carried, but was built until 1926. Late in 1928 the brothers then produced the fastest luxury large car ever built – the 6·9 litre Model J. Again this was a straight-eight, but this time with twin overhead camshafts and four valves per cylinder. The output was a claimed 265 bhp at 4,200 rpm, and the J would exceed 119 mph in top gear and reach 89 mph in second.

The J certainly rates amongst the world's finest and most beautiful cars. Its appearance was magnificent, with an elegant vee radiator with vertical slats, and bodies by the finest American coachbuilders such as Derham, Murphy and Le Baron, and by the great European *carrossiers*; 485 were built, and today the J is one of the most sought-after classic cars, commanding prices very much higher than its forbidding 1929 figure of around $17,500–$18,000 (£4,375–£4,500).

Left: *the car that inspired Enzo Ferrari with his love for twelve-cylinder engines – the racing version of the Packard 'Twin-Six' with which Ralph de Palma scored many successes in 1917–1919. With him here at Santa Monica is film star Douglas Fairbanks.*
Above: *Packard later switched to the straight-eight. This is a classic 1928 6·3 litre two-place convertible.*

Below: *a superbly prepared Show exhibit at Olympia, 1930, was the Daimler Double-Six chassis with 6½ litre aluminium V12 power unit, fluid flywheel and epicyclic gearbox.*

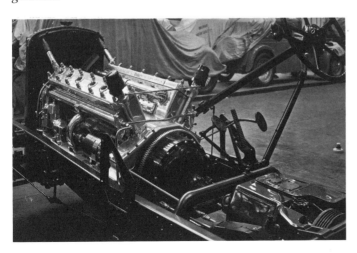

Rivals to Rolls

Many other makes, from many countries, aspired to rival these top makes. In Britain alone, Daimler, Napier, Lanchester and Leyland all catered for the same customers as Rolls-Royce, with varying success.

Daimler had the invaluable cachet of supplying cars to the Royal Family since the beginning of motoring. Their prestige models of the 1920s, the 7·4 litre 45hp and 4·9 litre 30hp, were sleeve-valve sixes of somewhat old-fashioned concept, offset by meticulous construction. The 5·7 litre 35hp with four-wheel brakes came in 1923, and in 1926 the famous Double-Six was introduced. Designed by L. H. Pomeroy, this had a 7·1 litre 60 degree V12 sleeve valve engine, with separate carburettor, distributor, contact breaker and magneto to each bank of cylinders, and a four-speed separate gearbox, in a chassis of three optional lengths, the biggest at 13ft 7in permitting the most spacious of coachwork. The Double Six was remarkably smooth and flexible, and would accelerate from 2mph to 82mph in top gear without apparent effort. Right at the close of the vintage era, Daimler introduced their fluid flywheel clutchless transmission with preselector control on the steering column.

Although Napier's new post-First World War product, a 6·2 litre 40/50 six, had an advanced aluminium

engine with steel cylinder liners and overhead camshaft valve operation, and a 4-speed gearbox in unit,
the firm were half-hearted about car production and
gave it up in 1924 to concentrate on aero engines.
Coincidentally, the Lanchester '40' also had a 6·2 litre
overhead camshaft six-cylinder engine, but this car,
product of one of the most enterprisingly original of
British marques right from 1895, differed from the
Napier in having a Lanchester patent three-speed

epicyclic gearbox, worm final drive and cantilever
rear springing.
  In quest of the utmost efficiency, Lanchester made
their own road springs, and preferred to build their
own coachwork. This was mounted on a rubber-
insulated sub-frame, and had cast alloy framing with
welded duralumin panels, a technique ten years
ahead of its time. Two wheel brakes sufficed on the
'40' until 1925, when a four-wheel servo-assisted

system was adopted. Not only did this superb car carry members of the Royal Family in supreme comfort, but in single-seater guise it lapped Brooklands track consistently at around 100mph, setting many long-distance records.

Luxury Bentleys

The name Bentley is usually associated with sports cars, but the 6½ litre introduced late in 1925 was more a high performance luxury car. Its 6,597cc 24-valve engine had a single overhead camshaft driven by three eccentric coupling rods giving silent, gear-less operation; it produced 140bhp at 3,500rpm, propelling the heaviest chassis and limousine coachwork in remarkable smoothness and silence at an effortless 75–80mph. Still more magnificent was the 8 litre, one of Britain's finest late-vintage creations, first seen at the 1930 Motor Show. Its 220bhp 7,983cc engine, an enlargement of the '6½', meant swift, silent acceleration and a 100mph maximum for the most elegant town carriage. One hundred 8 litre Bentleys were built before the Company was closed down in black 1931 and was subsequently taken over by Rolls-Royce.

Perhaps the most advanced (and expensive) of all

post-First World War British luxury cars was the Leyland Eight introduced at Olympia in 1920. Designed by Parry Thomas, with sheer perfection his avowed goal, it was Britain's first straight-eight. Its 7·3 litre monobloc engine had an overhead camshaft driven by eccentrics, hemispherical combustion chambers and leaf-type valve return springs; 145bhp was claimed on two carburettors at 2,500rpm. The four-speed gearbox was flexibly mounted, and the rear axle half-shafts were splayed to suit road camber. Other features were vacuum servo two-wheel brakes and torsion bars working in conjunction with cantilever rear springing.

The engine externals were beautifully machined and finished, but of the 18 Leylands built none could equal the best Rolls-Royce for sheer grace and symmetry of appearance. Building these costly superluxury cars proved a great embarrassment to Leyland Motors, overloaded at that time with commercial vehicle orders, and they suddenly stopped production in 1923. Parry Thomas left, taking as a present all remaining Leyland car parts, which he used to good effect by building them into the immensely successful Leyland-Thomas Brooklands track cars.

Another brief British contender for the luxury market was the Sheffield Simplex, a handsome car with the well-known designation '40/50' but a rather old-fashioned six cylinder engine with side valves and separate cylinders. It lasted until 1922, while the 38·4hp British Ensign scarcely lasted longer. This one had a modern 6·7 litre overhead camshaft six cylinder unit with aluminium block, a large conventional chassis and Rolls-like wire wheels. The larger Sunbeam models, such as the six cylinder overhead valve 24/70 with four wheel servo braking, and the later 5·4 litre 30/90 straight-eight, were cars of fine work-

Left: the gleaming aluminium 40/50 Rolls-Royce tourer almost dwarfs the two Mercedes-Benz, normally regarded as big cars. The centre one is a supercharged 6·8 litre S model with British coupe bodywork; the red car is a post-Vintage 380K.

Below: an historic French sports car, this 3½ litre overhead valve six-cylinder Lorraine-Dietrich is claimed to have won the 1925 Le Mans 24-hour race. It has been restored with incorrect mudguards and upholstery, and oversize tyres.

manship which drew a discerning if limited clientele during the 1920s.

Continental luxury

In Europe, Hispano-Suiza and Isotta-Fraschini had their rivals for the *grand luxe* market. The brothers Maurice and Henry Farman came fresh to automobile construction from the aircraft world in 1920, to build a really superb, expense-no-object car. It had the usual overhead camshaft engine, a six of 6·6 litres, with twin plugs per cylinder and twin carburettors. There were four speeds and four wheel brakes, compound suspension with both transverse leaf and cantilever springs, and aluminium bodywork. The Type A6B Farman had a 90mph maximum in open form; a true aristocrat among cars, it sold in small numbers until the 1931 depression.

Strangely, the great Renault company which produced thousands of bread-and-butter cars at keen prices also built a prestige model much used on State occasions. Called the 40CV 'Great Six' by the French, or the '45' in Britain, it had a huge, old-fashioned six cylinder side-valve engine of 9·1 litres, four speeds and a massive chassis with wooden wheels. The characteristic scuttle radiator held no less than 12 gallons of water! This monster weighed 2¾ tons, yet could attain 90mph – with a fuel consumption of around 8½ mpg.

Another veteran of the French industry, Panhard et Levassor, built small numbers of a large 7·4 litre sleeve-valve six, succeeded later by a 6·3 litre straight-eight, and both attracted some striking coachwork. Aviator Réné Fonck gave his name to another aspirant for the *haute classe* in automobiles, a 4·4 litre overhead camshaft eight which lasted until

Above: *a 'one-off' British sports car, this 7·2 litre Leyland Eight was built by Thomson and Taylor of Brooklands between 1927 and 1929, after Leyland Motors had disposed of all the parts of their luxury car project.*

Opposite page, far right: *the 1929 Renault Reinastella with 7·1 litre in-line eight-cylinder engine was a successor to the famous '45', and the first Renault with normal front-mounted radiator.* Right, top: *something of a wolf in sheep's clothing, this 1924 24/100/140 Mercedes saloon had a 6 litre supercharged engine.* Right: *a high-class Belgian car, the 1925 5·3 litre six-cylinder overhead-camshaft Excelsior 'Albert I' was big and heavy, but fast enough to win sports car races.*

Below: *a Delage D8, a French prestige car with 4 litre straight-eight overhead-valve engine.*

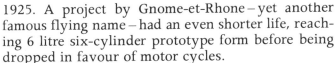

1925. A project by Gnome-et-Rhone – yet another famous flying name – had an even shorter life, reaching 6 litre six-cylinder prototype form before being dropped in favour of motor cycles.

But by far the most awe-inspiring luxury car to come from France was the so-called Golden Bugatti, which first appeared in 1927. Designed by Ettore Bugatti as the ultimate in cars for royalty and heads of state, the Type 41 'Royale' had the largest engine ever used in a European private car, a 12,750 cc bi-bloc straight-eight with overhead camshaft operating three valves per cylinder. Its 300 bhp (at 1,700 rpm) passed through a three-speed transmission on the rear axle, embodying a 'starter' gear, direct second on which the car could reach 80 mph, and overdrive top on which maximum speed was estimated at around 125 mph – if one could ever find roads suitable for this speed! The Golden Bugatti would motor at 3 mph in top gear and had a fuel consumption of between 5 and 8 mpg. Only seven were built.

Belgium contributed two very fine products, the 6 litre six cylinder sleeve-valved Minerva and a later 6·6 straight-eight which wore diverse makes of coachwork with much grace and elegance, and the Excelsior "Albert 1", named after its royal user, which had an advanced overhead cam six cylinder 5·4 litre engine, Adex servo braking, rear anti-roll bar and a formidable 90 mph-plus performance.

Despite domestic poverty German manufacturers, too, aspired to the Rolls-Royce class, and again the firms who essayed it had aircraft experience. Maybach, makers of aircraft and Zeppelin engines, built a large, luxurious 5·8 litre side-valve six in 1921, replacing it in 1926 with a 7 litre overhead valve model. In 1929 they produced a sensational 7 litre V12 cylinder car which was graced by the finest German coachwork.

Although in general the larger Mercedes products of the early 1920s were of sporting type, the 7·2 litre 28/95 six was occasionally clad in formal closed bodywork, while the later Type 630 with 6·2 litre six cylinder unit served as a limousine of distinct "wolf in sheep's clothing" character, having a supercharger which could be cut in at will, giving an output of 140 bhp and over 85 mph with surprising acceleration and an awe-inspiring blower scream. Late in 1930 the

No Vintage marque was more 'vintage' than Bentley,
founded in 1919 and closed down in 1931, to be taken over
subsequently by Rolls-Royce. Real Bentleys came in four
sizes, beginning with the beloved four-cylinder 3 litre,
epitome of the vintage sports car, followed in 1926 by
the $6\frac{1}{2}$ litre six which became the Speed Six, the $4\frac{1}{2}$ litre
four of 1927, and the 8 litre luxury six, built in the
firm's final year of existence. Bentley cars won the Le
Mans 24 Hours race five times in Vintage years, twice
with a 3 litre, once with a $4\frac{1}{2}$, and twice with the Speed
Six, and it was bitter fortune that this fine British make
was allowed to perish in the Depression.
Below: a circa 1924 example of the 3 litre Bentley,
wearing red as a change from the customary British green.
Right: a fine cutaway drawing of one of the famous
1929–30 $4\frac{1}{2}$ litre 'Blower' Bentleys, specifically developed
with Amherst Villiers superchargers by Sir Henry Birkin
for racing at Le Mans and elsewhere.
Opposite, below: a normal but very resplendent $4\frac{1}{2}$ litre
engine with twin carburetters.

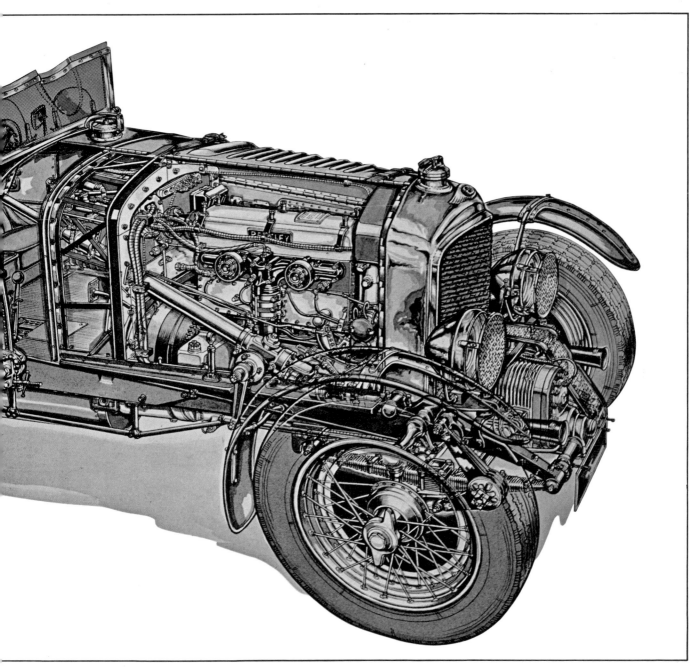

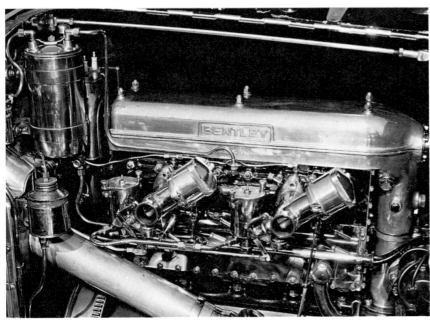

Grosser Mercedes with 7·6 litre motor *mit kompressor* which could be engaged at will, transported German diplomats and politicians including future Chancellor Adolf Hitler at speeds of up to 100mph in comfort and dignity.

Performing a similar task in Austria was the Viennese-built Graf und Stift six-seater limousine, with a big 7·7 litre six cylinder engine, which was succeeded in 1930 by a 6 litre overhead camshaft straight-eight. Czechoslovakia's "Rolls-Royce", the 6·6 litre six-cylinder overhead valve Skoda of 1923–25, was more correctly their 'Hispano-Suiza', being built under licence from the Spanish/French concern with Czech bodywork fitted.

In Italy Fiat made a brief bid for the luxury market with a very advanced car, the Tipo 520 Super-Fiat, shown at Paris in 1921 in coupé de ville form. Its 6·8 litre 60 degree vee-twelve cylinder engine with over-head valves gave over 80bhp at 2,200rpm. It had a three-speed gearbox, four-wheel brakes, and steel-spoked Sankey wheels which rather marred its elegance. After building a few Super-Fiats the makers decided not to put it into full production.

The Spanish Elizalde 50/60 Type 48 limousine, which astonished visitors to the same 1921 Paris Salon by its enormous size, was powered by an 8 litre straight eight overhead valve engine with twin bronze heads and a claimed 250bhp. The car was over 22 feet long and had rear semi-elliptic springs supple-

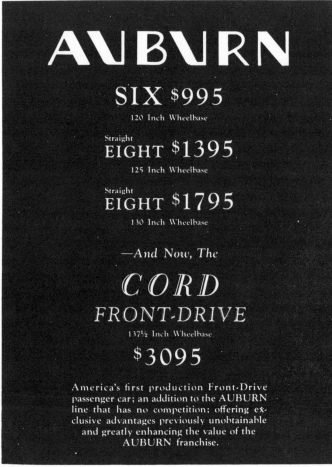

American aspirants to the 'Rolls-Royce' class included the Pierce-Arrow (top left), a car which like modern Jaguars bore no nameplate, the makers holding that discerning observers could always recognise it without a label. This 1921 Model 38 was a big 24-valve six of conservative design but impeccable workmanship.
Left: the Auburn-Duesenberg combine which launched the controversial front wheel drive 5 litre eight-cylinder Cord in 1929.

Above: Cadillac were American pioneers in the use of V8 engines. This is the 5½ litre Series 341 'de ville' town carriage of 1928.

Below: an idealistic American car, superbly made but expensive, was the Wills St. Claire. Last of the line, this 1926 model had an ohc six-cylinder power unit.

mented by a pair of cantilevers; such a behemoth did not long survive, and subsequent Elizalde cars were of more manageable proportions.

American quality

Cadillac, Packard and Duesenberg did not have things all their own way in the top quality market, Lincoln, Peerless, Pierce-Arrow and Cunningham being at least four of their rivals. Only Lincoln, ''Ford's prestige line'', survives today, yet it was founded by Henry M.Leland, a former Cadillac designer. He evolved the Lincoln 5·8 litre side-valve V8 but ran out of money in the depression of 1920–21, whereupon Henry Ford bought the company and continued its production as a large, luxury car. A Lincoln was used by the US President in 1924, and the marque has served the State almost ever since.

Peerless, that very fine American make, followed Cadillac's lead in 1915 by marketing a V8 which lasted until 1924. Pierce-Arrow stuck to an in-line six but gave it four valves per cylinder. It was a dated design otherwise, but built to the most rigorous standards; Pierce-Arrows were always distinguished from other cars in having curious headlights integral with the mudguards. In 1929 Studebaker took over, introducing a new 6·2 litre straight-eight, but even a new 7 litre 150bhp 12-cylinder in 1932 could not save this former aristocrat. The Rochester-built Cunning-ham was consistently a 6-litre V8 through the vintage era, finely made, expensive and exclusive.

THE VINTAGE SPORTS CAR

'We were going to make a fast car, a good car, the best in its class...'

W. O. Bentley

The tremendous zest for enjoyment and adventure which was a logical sequence to the First World War had its effect, not merely on the quantity, but also the kinds of car that were built after the Armistice. Not every customer wanted a staid, inexpensive tourer, nor did every manufacturer wish to build it. Youth wanted cars with speed and dash, and many engineers with pride and enthusiasm for their work wanted to make good cars that worked well, not merely dull, profitable cars. Fortunately there was still scope in the 1920s for such idealists, whose interest frequently turned toward the sports car, where an enthusiastic clientele encouraged good design, workmanship and performance.

The immortal Frazer Nash, in this case a 1925 Anzani-engined Boulogne model, in action at a speed trial.

Not that their way was easy, for cold boardroom minds seldom enthused, save over high profit and low expenditure, and could not always grasp that quality and sound design paid off in the long run. W.O.Bentley said that his worst day of the month was the regular board meeting. "There were always those who would niggle and nag, demanding economies, constantly pressing for the second-rate for a car we were to advertise and sell as the finest in its class, opposing the expenditure of money on vital equipment". This was one of the problems of starting a new make with more enthusiasm than capital; Alvis, Aston Martin, HE, Eric Campbell, Silver Hawk and other post-war sporting marques ran into similar difficulties.

Older manufacturers had a better chance, for their factories and their reputations were already established. Thus Vauxhall of Luton, blessed with a brilliant designer in L.H.Pomeroy, rated the premier sports car makers at the opening of the vintage era, with their famous 30/98 E-type. Basically this was a pre-war design, evolved as a 'one-off' for speed hill-climbing. Its $4\frac{1}{2}$ litre four-cylinder, fixed head, side-valve engine still lived in an Edwardian sub-frame, but it gave 90 willing horsepower at 2,800rpm, which

Right, above: *the Austin Swallow, a neat special-bodied Austin Seven, was produced by William (later Sir William) Lyons from 1927 to 1932, before he founded Jaguar.*
Right: *one of France's prettiest vintage sports cars was the 1 litre four-cylinder Amilcar 'Surbaisse'.*

meant 85 mph in handsome open Velox form, with excellent low-speed flexibility and somewhat doubtful brakes. They called it a 'fast touring car' in 1920, the term 'sports car' not having been invented then, but undoubtedly the 30/98 was the first inter-wars example of the genus.

In 1923 it was given overhead valves and 112 bhp despite a capacity cut to 4,224cc; this model was designated the OE. It was endowed with front brakes a year later. Vauxhall even tried a hydraulic system in 1926, but brakes remained a 30/98 inadequacy right to 1927, when the marque moved under the General Motors umbrella and vacated the sporting scene.

Enter Bentley

Unlike the Vauxhall 30/98, the Bentley was all new in 1919, when W.O.Bentley, a clever engineer, aero-engine designer and pre-War racing driver, his brother H.M., and a talented hardcore of engineers built the first 3 litre in a mews garage off Baker Street, in London. 'W.O.' intended the design to be right, with no compromise, and capital resources creaked getting it to the production stage. The 80 × 149mm,

The superbly balanced curves of mudguards and body on this 1924 four-wheel braked OE Vauxhall 30/98 with Wensum coachwork make it one of the most handsome as well as one of the finest performers among Vintage sports cars.

four cylinder engine had 16 valves in a fixed head, operated by a shaft-driven overhead camshaft, and gave around 70 bhp. Allied to a separate four-speed gearbox with ideal ratios the result was 75 mph with remarkable tractability and good handling.

Moreover the Bentley was most attractively balanced in appearance, with a handsome vee radiator set well back, wire wheels and rakish body lines with swept mudguards. Production began in 1921 at Cricklewood and every car had a five year

Starting a reputation: the now world-famous Le Mans 24 Hours race began in 1923, when despite many troubles John Duff's privately-entered 3 litre Bentley finished 5th, presaging five striking victories in the next seven years.

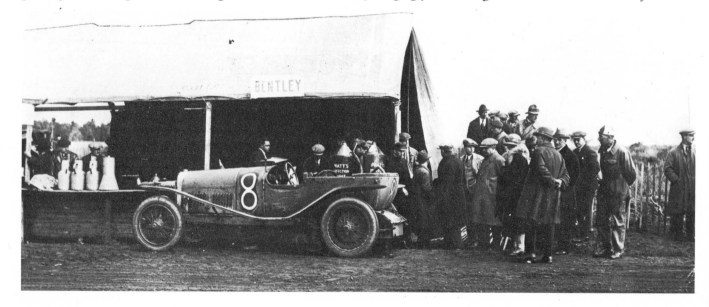

guarantee – a confidence more than justified, for such were the 3 litre's reserves of strength that of the 1620 examples built between 1921 and 1928, over 400 survive today, and many of them are still raced.

The range was augmented in 1926 by the $6\frac{1}{2}$ litre mentioned in Chapter 5 – a superb luxury machine of such performance that, in short chassis 'Speed Six' form, it won the Le Mans 24-hour Race twice running; in 1927 by the larger four-cylinder $4\frac{1}{2}$ litre destined to replace the 3 litre; and in 1930 by the awe-inspiring six-cylinder 8 litre.

Ettore Bugatti's well-known jibe at Bentley, making "Europe's fastest lorries", suggests that vintage Bentleys only last so long because they are built so massively. Certainly W.O.Bentley's philosophy was to use large, lightly worked engines, but his chassis were designed for the severe stresses of the time, when roads were poor and automobile engineering had not progressed beyond the channel section chassis requiring high beam strength, suspended by non-independent semi-elliptic leaf springs.

The quality and stamina of the cars aside, it was racing that made Bentley. Some say it also broke them, but this is questionable; their five famous victories at Le Mans, and others elsewhere, cost them an amazingly small outlay, and in their most successful year, 1929, when they placed 1–2–3–4 at Le Mans and won two major British races, racing cost Bentley Motors only £2,487. The end was brutally sudden: a £65,000 debt, nothing unusual in that time of depression, some biased advice to the main source of finance, and a receiver was appointed in 1931, and Britain's greatest sports car of the time had died. Bentleys' living memorial is the amazing number still around today, hale and hearty.

The 1500s

Another revered vintage name, Alvis, also owes its longevity to an unrelenting policy of sound construction. Like Bentley, it began in 1919, founded by T.G.John whose first model, the 10/30, had a willing 1,460cc side-valve four-cylinder engine designed by G.F.H.de Freville, maker of a wartime aluminium piston called the 'Alvis'. John acquired rights to the name and the engine. The 10/30 grew progressively into the 11/40 and then the 12/40. Next came the finest vintage Alvis of all, the overhead valve 12/50 of 1923–32, designed by Capt. Smith-Clarke.

Strong without being heavy, with a fine four-speed gearbox, and a maximum speed of 75mph, the $1\frac{1}{2}$ litre 12/50 Alvis with its famous aluminium 'duck's back' two seater body proved highly successful. It scored countless competition wins, including a sensational 93·29mph victory, in stripped and tuned form, in the 1923 200 Miles Race at Brooklands.

Front brakes were fitted from 1925, touring versions were also built, and 12/50 quality is testified by the existence today of over 300 in good running order. Alvis built other models in the 1920s, such as the six-cylinder Silver Eagle and the front wheel drive cars with overhead camshaft four- and eight-cylinder engines and all-independent suspension. Such bold-

Classic car, classic event, of Vintage days – an Alvis 12/50 aluminium 'Duck's back' super-sports with rakish outside exhaust tackling Beggars' Roost, one of the hardest climbs in the 1925 London-Land's End Trial.

ness in conservative times almost broke the Company, until they reverted quickly to the more classic layout.

Two other British sports cars of widely differing kinds were the Aston Martin and the Frazer Nash. The former marque was launched by Lionel Martin and Robert Bamford with a rival to the $1\frac{1}{2}$ litre Bugatti, the 1919–20 car with a reworked Coventry Simplex side valve engine, four wheel brakes, rear fuel tank and graceful aluminium bodywork. Being virtually hand-made it was expensive, but it per-

Sunbeam's sports 3 litre twin-cam six appeared in 1925, when one driven by Chassagne and S.C.H. Davis (seen here) placed second at Le Mans. Chassis limitations offset good engine performance, and few 3 litres were built.

Left: *Vintage masterpiece by designer Vittorio Jano was the Alfa Romeo 6C 1500 Super Sport of 1928–29. This lithe and graceful Italian sports car had a jewel-like 1½ litre six-cylinder engine with twin overhead camshafts and a Roots-type supercharger, giving 84bhp at 5000rpm, resulting in extreme liveliness and a maximum speed of close on 100mph. The bodywork with its characteristic flared wings was generally by Zagato, and few late-Vintage sports cars remain more desirable. A 1750cc version appeared in 1929, and these inspiring Alfa Romeos won many sports car races.*

Below: *one of the better light cars of the early Vintage era was the 11·9hp 1½ litre AC, powered by the well-known Anzani four-cylinder side-valve engine, and with a three-speed gearbox on the rear axle, embodying an unusual transmission disc brake. Never the cheapest in its class, the model's qualities were emphasised by many successes in trials, races, hillclimbs and record breaking.*

formed very well, with good handling and braking; 69 had been sold when finances ran out in 1925. A year later Renwick and Bertelli re-established Aston Martin with a fine new 1½ litre model with overhead camshaft four-cylinder engine and underslung final drive. A short-wheelbase 'S' model with underslung chassis was developed into the famous dry-sump International, variants of which ran at Le Mans with ever-mounting success from 1928 well into the 1930s.

The Frazer Nash was unique. Born in 1924 when Archie Frazer Nash foresaw the end of the cyclecar and left GN, it retained a basically GN chassis and suspension, and the three-speed chain final drive through sprockets and dog clutches, and was marketed in 1925 with a 1½ litre side valve Anzani engine. This had the modest output of 40bhp, but in a skimpy 13cwt car this was enough to give a maximum speed of over 70mph, with prodigious acceleration. All 'Nashes were virtually hand-built to order for members of 'the Chain Gang', as owners were called. In 1928 the Aldington brothers took over, replaced the Anzani with a Meadows overhead valve engine, fitted four speeds, and continued building these inspiring sports cars well into the 1930s.

Riley's first sports car was the 1923 Redwing, distinguished by its raffish open two-seater body in fashionable polished aluminium with long, swept, red-painted wings. 1926 brought the trend-setting Riley Nine with advanced twin high-cam overhead valve engine, and a potential which attracted Parry Thomas and Reid Railton. They evolved a low chassis, high performance 'Brooklands' sports model, offering 80mph for £395 in 1928, and from this sprang a whole generation of high-efficiency sporting Rileys.

A distinguished marque descended from a production car was M.G., launched by Cecil Kimber of Morris Garages Ltd in 1924. Kimber started from a tuned Morris Oxford 'Bullnose' tourer, but in 1928 two new M.G.s were introduced – the 18/80 overhead camshaft six and the first Midget, the M type. Based on the little 847cc overhead camshaft Morris Minor, this wore a shapely little open-two-seater fabric body, and cost just £165.

So successful was the Midget in those tight times that it swept the 14/40 and 18/80 out of existence, and also precipitated M.G. into a highly successful racing and record breaking programme. Its chief rival was, of course, the 747cc Austin Seven, which with expert tuning and ultra-lightweight bodywork, was extremely fast. The supercharged 'Ulster' Austin introduced in 1928 weighed less than 1,000lb and its 33bhp

Famous British sports cars Top: *Kaye Don's supercharged 1½ litre Meadows-engined Lea-Francis 'Hyper' winning the 1928 Ulster TT race; behind comes Dutilleux's Bugatti.*
Centre: *the simple but effective six-cylinder pushrod ohv Talbot 90 and 105 models made a big impact in sports car racing in 1930–32.*
Right: *the famous 1½ litre Redwing Riley of 1923.*

could propel it at 80mph. It cost £225!

There were many more. . . . The rakish A.B.C. of 1920–25 with 1,200cc aircooled flat twin engine, its overhead valve heads protruding each side of the bonnet, four speeds and a stimulating power to weight ratio; the 1½ litre Lea-Francis with Meadows engine, supercharged as the Hyper with attractive sloping radiator and renowned as the 1928 Ulster TT winner; and the Lagonda, which 'went sporting' in 1925 with a 2 litre high-camshaft car which grew into a supercharged Speed Model by 1928 and a 3 litre pushrod overhead valve six by 1929. These cars wore handsome open four-seater fabric bodies with elegant swept wings, and were copied both by Hillman on their Husky sports and Bean on the 14/70 Hadfield Bean of 1929–30.

There was also the 1930 ultra-low '100mph' Invicta with 4½ litre Meadows engine, never as fast as its superb appearance suggested but a great rally performer; the ultra-high Talbot 90 of the same year, never as slow as its build and 2·2 litre pushrod overhead valve six-cylinder engine suggested, and with a vigorous racing career ahead of it; the H.E., a high-quality 2 litre side-valve which had a Bentley lifespan from 1920 to 1931; the pleasant little 950cc Gwynne of 1922–26, with overhead valve engine, 65mph underfoot, and a 'hipbath' body; and still others in a creative, enthusiastic decade when high performance meant a spirited, pulsating overhead valve engine, a good crash gearbox, 90mph, and roads where these qualities could still be enjoyed.

Continental sports cars

The same zest for fast motoring and enjoyment prevailed across the Channel in the 1920s, when cars of different nationalities seemed to strongly echo national characteristics. French and Italian cars had a Latin energy and excitability, while Germany's sports models were Teutonically stolid and efficient.

With her long, straight roads, France had always built big, powerful *grands routiers*, and if these were not specifically known as sports cars before the First World War, they were their true antecedents. A vigorous new generation appeared after the War; cars such as the Hispano-Suiza, which gave sports car performance regardless of its bodywork; big 'long-legged' Panhards, Voisins and Peugeots with sleeve valves, and fast, nimble four- and six-cylinder Delages.

Chenard-Walcker was another of France's great vintage sporting marques, building cars with zestful overhead camshaft engines in four and eight cylinder

Rival 'babies': the special sporting Austin Seven (above) is the supercharged 32bhp 'Ulster', so-called after two placed 3rd and 4th in the TT, winning their class. The MG Midget (left), evolved from the 1929 847cc Morris Minor, became Britain's most popular sports car during the next few years, while special 750cc supercharged versions won many races. This standard M-type Midget completed the 1930 Monte Carlo Rally.

forms from 2 to 4 litres, in strong, four-wheel braked chassis. A Chenard-Walcker 3 litre won the first Le Mans 24 Hours race in 1923, while in 1925 Chenard took up full-width streamlining on the famous 1,100cc 'tank' which won countless races and easily topped 100mph when supercharged. Lorraine-Dietrich twice won at Le Mans, in 1925 and 1926, with a superb 3½ litre overhead valve six which had servo four-wheel braking. Worthy rivals included the Georges Irat 2 litre fours and 3 litre sixes and the 3 litre four-cylinder Ariès with ultra-light wooden bodywork which so nearly won Le Mans 1927 instead of Bentley.

The 'Sammy': a 1927 Model G 1100cc four-cylinder twin-cam French Salmson storms a grade in the Land's End Trial.
Right: *Hans Stuck with his magnificent 1930 Austro-Daimler ADR6, prototype of the 3·6 litre 'Bergmeister', named in honour of his 1930 European Mountain Championship.*

Bugatti
The Bugatti was the outstanding French sports car of those years, a nimble, superbly balanced, exquisitely engineered creation that evokes world-wide admira-

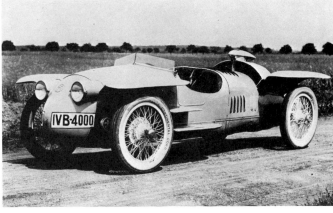

The Lancia Lambda was far ahead of its time with independent front suspension, integral construction and compact V4 engine. Here is one of three which scored a 1-2-3 class win in the 1924 'Bad Roads Race', near Lille.

Still more advanced was the Rumpler-designed sports two-seater Benz 'Tropfenwagen' ('teardrop car') of 1924, with mid-located 2 litre six-cylinder twin-cam engine, independent rear swing axles and inboard rear brakes.

tion today. Designed by Italian-born Ettore Bugatti and built at Molsheim in Alsace-Lorraine, the marque with the distinctive horseshoe radiator leapt into post-war prominence with the Type 22 1½ litre four-cylinder 16-valve single-cam 'Brescia', equipped with the delicate looking semi-elliptic front and reversed quarter-elliptic rear springing which set a pattern for all subsequent Bugatti suspensions.

The first Bugatti straight eight appeared in 1922, the 2 litre Type 30, and in 1924 came the famous Type 35, a racing-cum-sports car of unmatched elegance in design and form. Its engine was a single-cam 2 litre straight eight with three valves per cylinder, and the car had Bugatti's unique aluminium-alloy eight-spoked wheels. Apart from the less expensive four-cylinder 1½ litre Type 37, all subsequent Bugattis had straight eight engines, ranging from the 2 litre Type 38 to the 2·3 Type 43, the 3 litre plain bearing Type 44, 3·3 Type 49, 5·3 Type 46 and the powerful supercharged 4·9 twin-camshaft Type 50 of late 1930.

The French excelled in the small sports car class, with cars such as the Salmson and Amilcar. Both were four-cylinder 1100s, the Salmsons indulging in twin overhead camshafts and optional supercharging, while Amilcars contrived to emulate Salmson performance with side valve engines. Both wore pretty pointed tail two-seater bodies and were very popular in Britain. Broadly similar 1100s such as Senéchal, BNC, Rally and EHP also flowered, then withered in those stormy economic days.

One tends to associate Mercedes of Germany with vast six cylinder machinery, but their 1922 1½ litre four cylinder sports car was equally important, being the first to be commercially offered in Europe with a supercharger. This was a Roots vertical type engaged at will by full depression of the accelerator, and the same system was adopted by Dr Porsche on his ponderous 6·2 litre 33/180K, and subsequent 6·7 litre 36/220 and 7·1 litre 38/250 six cylinder Mercedes-Benz (the two makes combined in 1926). These vast but superbly proportioned cars, with their three great exhaust pipes sprouting from the bonnet and the arrogant vee radiator, epitomised the 'great white Mercedes' of motoring legend, giving sheer brute power uninhibited by trivia such as size, noise or cost.

Three from Italy. Top: *a handsome 1925 22/90 Alfa Romeo RLSS two-seater with 3 litre six-cylinder pushrod overhead valve engine.* Left: *the 1930 3·7 litre six-cylinder side-valve Fiat 525SS with dashing spider body by Viotti.* Above: *a lively 1½ litre sports four was the OM Tipo 469, which had side valves but a special Ricardo cylinder head.*

Other German makes such as NAG, Simson-Supra and Durkopp built interesting sports cars to the design conventions of the time, while the Porsche-designed Austro-Daimler from Austria, which had a six cylinder overhead camshaft engine, was an outstanding performer.

One German car of the period was prophetically unorthodox – the 1924 2 litre Benz. This had a six-cylinder twin overhead camshaft engine at the rear, independent rear springing and inboard brakes, and streamlined open two seater bodywork. In the stereotyped 1920s, however, this highly original design fell on stony ground.

In Italy the rising marque of the 1920s was Alfa Romeo, advancing spectacularly under the spur of racing. They began with the RL series of 3 litre sixes in 1922, a special version of which won the 1923 Targa Florio, then followed in 1925 with their first overhead camshaft model, the 1½ litre six cylinder 6C 1500 designed by Vittorio Jano. This was rapidly evolved into the 54 bhp twin-cam Sport and the 76 bhp supercharged Super Sport; 1,750cc versions appeared in 1929. These sixes were 'naturals' for international sports car racing, which apart from Le Mans they largely dominated.

By 1930 Alfa Romeo were looking ahead to straight-eights, but the twin-cam sixes with their racey spider bodywork and swept wings possessed a feline grace

typifying the Italian sports car of the late 1920s, and much imitated elsewhere. Other cars such as the side-valve O.M., Diatto and Maserati followed in the wake of Alfa Romeo, while the lively overhead camshaft Fiat 509 fitted with various special bodies dominated the cheaper market. One very important design was not even intended as a sports car – the Lancia Lambda of 1922. With a composite chassis/body, independent front springing with hydraulic damping, and narrow-angle V4 engine, the Lambda was a car years ahead of its time, esteemed for its roadholding and handling.

The Americans

Europe's enthusiasm for sports cars was not echoed in the USA, where most manufacturers sought merely to meet the feverish demand for basic transport rather than cater for a very minor sector. The mini-slump of 1920–21 further reduced the ranks of the enthusiastic makers, and although Mercer, one of the greatest of pre-First World War American sports cars builders, was merged with a group which also acquired two other great makes, Locomobile and Simplex, it lived only until 1925. The famous prewar 'Raceabout' was revived as a Series 5 4·9 litre side-valve four with the famous exposed cylindrical fuel tank, wire wheels, side doors and domed wings. In 1923 came the less exciting 5·4 litre six-cylinder Rochester-engined Series 6, and two years later the end. Mercer's legendary rival had always been the Stutz, and whereas, according to the muse, Mercer fans said:

> ''You'd have to be nutz
> To drive a Stutz'',

their rivals retorted:

> ''You couldn't do worser
> Than buy a Mercer''.

Alas, like Mercer, Stutz rather lost direction after the war when founder Harry C. Stutz left the firm. In 1926, however, the company had a keen new proprietor in Fred Moscovics, who quickly had it producing a new 90 bhp, 16-plug overhead cam straight-eight of 4·7 litres, with hydraulic brakes and underslung final drive. Soon a Black Hawk 'Speedster' 4·9 litre variant appeared, and two Frenchmen raced one at Le Mans in 1928, scoring a brilliant second place against the Bentleys.

This should have offset the much-publicised defeat of a Stutz at Indianapolis by a Hispano-Suiza in a special 24 hour challenge race earlier that year, but in the 1920s Le Mans meant nothing to the Americans and decline set in for Stutz. They fought back in 1929 with an exciting short-chassis 5·3 litre model for which they revived the grand old name 'Bearcat', one

placing 5th at Le Mans. Their death throes came just beyond vintage bounds, after the introduction of a classic twin overhead cam 32-valve 5·3 litre model called the DV32.

The line between sports and sporting cars is difficult to define on American cars. The great 6·8 litre twin-cam eight cylinder Duesenberg J introduced in 1928 really belongs in both categories. It generally carried elegant bodywork and was thus very heavy, but the claimed 265 bhp – in truth nearer 207 – flung it along at close on 120mph. Two associates of Duesenberg were Auburn and Cord, the former marketing an attractive straight-eight boat-tailed two-seater Speedster in around 1924. The Cord was pure sensation in 1929, having a 4·9 eight cylinder engine driving the front wheels, and the most sporting lines ever for something not claiming to be a true sports car, with vee radiator set well back, low build and long swept wings.

Kissel, another sport-minded American make, began with a 4·3 litre side valve six-cylinder open model nick-named the 'Gold Bug' by reason of its yellow finish. Soon Lycoming engines replaced Kissel's own, and the pointed tail 'White Eagle' speedster of 1929 had optional 3, 3·4 or 4·9 litre in-line eight-cylinder units. The Du Pont was a rarer, costlier rival; the rakish Model G speedster of 1928 was powered by a 5·3 litre eight-cylinder Continental engine, and looking like a triple-sized Amilcar! Both Kissel and Du Pont died in the depression.

An American on the Continent (right) *one of the 4·1 litre six-cylinder Chrysler '72's which did so well at Le Mans in 1928, placing 3rd and 4th.*

An American with the Continental touch, the 1930 Jordan 'Speedway' (below) *had a 5·3 litre straight-eight engine and styling* à la Hispano-Suiza. *Cost killed it in 1931.*

RACING AND RECORDS

'Every man who steps into anybody's automobile owes his life to automobile racing...'

Homer McKee, writing of Indianapolis, 1922

The post-war stimulus in general motoring also infected motor racing. America revived her Indianapolis 500 Miles race in May 1919, and at Brooklands racing resumed early in 1920. The Automobile Club de France (ACF) took another year to revive their august Grand Prix, much to the annoyance of the French manufacturer Ernest Ballot, who was anxious to prove his fine new eight cylinder cars before his countrymen. The race took place in July 1921 on an unsealed, stone-strewn course at Le Mans. To the horror of the French, it was won by the invading American team of straight-eight, hydraulic-braked 3 litre Duesenbergs, after the leading Ballot retired with a stone through its petrol tank.

In National colours. Above: *a 1924 2 litre four-cylinder supercharged 'Targa Florio'-type Mercedes in authentic German white, restored for competition use in Britain.*

Left: *a handsome 1928 2 litre supercharged straight-eight Maserati in glorious Italian red. The Brooklands silencer without fishtail looks incongruous on this well-restored car, today in the Biscaretti Museum at Turin.*

Three months later the first Italian Grand Prix was held at Brescia, and although Ballot was avenged when his cars took the first two places, the ACF were horrified: not only had their French Grand Prix lost its exclusive status, but the Brescia organisers actually paid out prize money! With growing professionalism, however, this was to become a regular feature of racing.

The 1922–25 period, when the top limit allowed by the Grand Prix Formula was reduced from 3 to 2 litres, saw the beginning of an intensive era of technical development, in which Italy, Britain and France all played an important part. Sixes, fours, eights and V12s all appeared, all with twin overhead camshafts, but the straight-eight eventually emerged the firm favourite. Fiat won both the French and Italian GPs of 1922 with six cylinder cars, then shattered everyone in the 1923 French GP at Tours by fielding straight-eights equipped with vane-type superchargers. The opposition couldn't see the Italian cars for dust, but that same dust choked their superchargers and forced them out one by one, giving the race to the British Sunbeams which, ironically, were copies of the older six cylinder Fiat! Three months later Fiat had changed their vane blowers for Roots type and triumphed in the Italian GP at Monza.

More irony followed in the 1924 Grand Prix, when Fiat, Sunbeam and Bugatti fell by the wayside, and the upstart new racing marque from Milan, Alfa Romeo, won with a supercharged straight-eight very like the 1923 Fiat! Irony became tragedy in the 1925 race, when Alfa Romeo's dashing number one driver

Antonio Ascari tangled fatally with the paling fence at Montlhéry, his team mates withdrew, and victory fell to the V12 Delages. The four-year 2 litre Formula brought new Grands Prix in Spain and Belgium, and France's classic diminished progressively in importance, becoming just one of several races in a series.

Degeneration

International interest waned with a new $1\frac{1}{2}$ litre formula in 1926–27, when the Grands Prix became a struggle between three French makes, Delage, Bugatti and Talbot-Darracq, all with supercharged straight-eights of exquisite but costly design. Bugatti snatched two early wins in the European Grand Prix in Spain and a farcical 1926 French Grand Prix, which was contested by three Bugattis! Then Delage found their feet and became invincible. They won the first British Grand Prix, held at Brooklands, and in 1927 won four races in a row – the French, Spanish, European (Italian) and British Grands Prix, all with the same driver, Robert Benoist.

Further deterioration followed in 1928 when the authorities freed engine size but imposed weight limits, and only one race, the European Grand Prix at Monza was run to the rules. It fell to Chiron in a Bugatti, but the race was marred by a terrible accident when Materassi's Talbot crashed into the crowd, and 22 spectators as well as the driver were killed. The French Grand Prix was a dull sports car affair won by a Bugatti. In 1929 the situation was even worse, with the French Grand Prix an uninspiring fuel consumption race won by the inevitable Bugatti. Elsewhere free formula events were run, among them the sensational new Monaco Grand

The '500' (above) *lap 1 of the Indianapolis 500 Miles, America's greatest race, with a 5 litre Ballot leading. The Grand Prix* (below) *start of the 1922 French GP at Strasbourg, with winner Felice Nazarro (Fiat) in the foreground.*

Prix, which was actually held in the winding streets of Monte Carlo and grew into a unique classic.

The Grand Prix situation cheered up somewhat in 1930, the final vintage year, with the appearance of a new challenger from Italy, the 2½ litre straight-eight supercharged Maserati, which won five races. It missed the French Grand Prix, which was wisely switched at short notice to free formula regulations and went to Etancelin's Bugatti, hounded home, amazingly, by Englishman 'Tim' Birkin's massive 4½ litre supercharged Le Mans Bentley, stripped of mudguards and lights. It was the last time such a thing could happen in a Grand Prix, for with the 1930s came a full professional renaissance.

Sports car racing is born

An important development in the vintage years was the growth of races for sports cars. Actually these were termed 'production touring cars' at first, and the class became popular with the public as being much closer to "the cars you can buy" than Grand Prix machinery. With such races split into numerous capacity classes, each furnishing a "winner", the car, fuel, oil and equipment manufacturers liked them too. The first event, the somewhat remote Corsican Grand Prix over a gruelling mountain course on that Mediterranean isle, came in April 1921 and was won by Guyot in a 3 litre Bignan. The Boillot Cup at Boulogne followed, falling to Dubonnet's great 8 litre Hispano-Suiza, and the success of these two races set off a series of Touring Grands Prix as supporting events to the French Grand Prix, the first at Strasbourg in 1922 going to a Voisin.

A Belgian sports car Grand Prix was also held in

'The Boards' (below) *high-speed racing on short oval wooden banked tracks was highly popular in the USA in Vintage days. Speeds of well over 100mph were regularly attained. Here a Miller Durant Special leads at the Fresno 1-mile speedway, California, in 1923.*

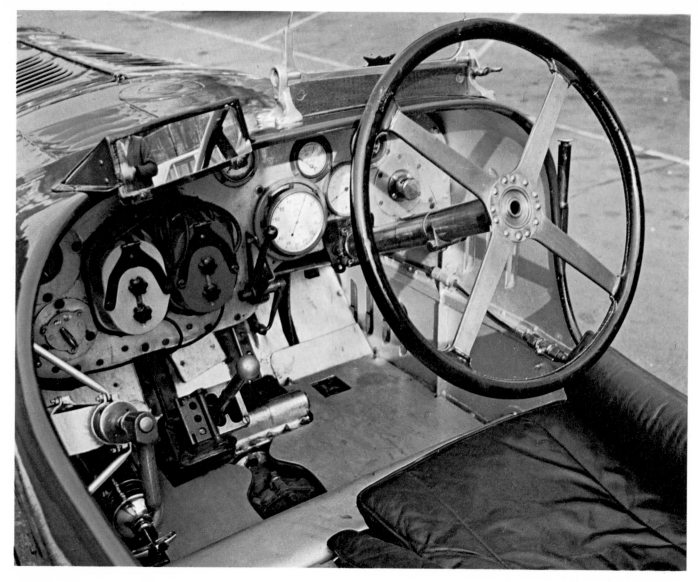

1922 at Spa, while the *Circuit des Routes Pavees*, or 'Bad Roads Race' was an inspired piece of opportunism by Lille motor clubs to use war-torn cobbled roads for a race without the expense of re-making them; as a unique test of stamina in cars and drivers it survived until 1931. The year 1923 brought 24-hour racing to Europe, first in the Bol d'Or for small cars, then at Le Mans, where the Grand Prix d'Endurance has grown through the years to world pre-eminence. The first Le Mans race drew 33 starters, all French except one 3-litre Bentley driven by Duff and Clement. A 3-litre Chenard-Walcker won, the Bentley being fifth after holing its fuel tank.

The same two drivers in the same Bentley outraged the French the following year by winning the Le Mans race outright. French Lorraine-Dietrich cars won in 1925 and 1926, after which the great green Bentleys from Britain scored their epic "four wins in a row" from 1927 to 1930. The 1927 race was particularly dramatic when two of the three Bentleys were eliminated in a multiple crash, while the third, also involved, was extracted battered but unbowed to be jury-repaired and win the race, driven by S.C.H.Davis and Dr Benjafield.

By then sports car racing had spread all over Europe. In Italy town-to-town racing was revived in 1927 with the dramatic Mille Miglia. This ran from Brescia to Brescia in a giant 1,000 mile figure-of-eight route crossing at Bologna. The first race proved an unexpected 1–2–3 triumph for the 2 litre side-valve OM team, but from 1928 on the race was very much an Alfa Romeo benefit.

In 1928 the RAC Tourist Trophy, dormant since 1922, was revived as a sports car contest in Northern Ireland. The 13·6 mile Ards circuit outside Belfast brought some tremendous racing, and Kaye Don in a 1½ litre supercharged Lea-Francis was the 1928 winner from an Alvis. In 1929 foreign competition was attracted, and the German Rudolf Caracciola won on wet roads in a big 7·1 litre Mercedes-Benz, defeating Alfa Romeo, while in 1930 the Alfas played with the opposition to score a 1–2–3 victory.

Britain also tried long-distance racing, although the 'Double Twelve' races were a pale shadow of Le Mans, being held at Brooklands where night racing was forbidden, and being split into two 12-hour runs. Alfa Romeo just beat Bentley in 1929, but the huge Speed Six Bentleys scored 1–2 in 1930. Yet another new sports car race in 1929 was the Irish Grand Prix, held in Dublin's Phoenix Park. Again Alfa Romeo

A great British name in Vintage racing days, Sunbeam, won the French GP in 1923 and lost in 1924 owing to magneto defects. Above: the engine of a surviving 1924 2 litre GP car, its Roots supercharger wearing a non-standard SU carburetter. Left: the riding mechanic's view. Below: with two GP blocks on a special crankcase the potent Sunbeam 4 litre V12 broke the land speed record in 1926 at 152·33mph, while in 1930 Kaye Don (seen at the wheel) lapped Brooklands at a record 137·58mph.

won, but in 1930 Caracciola, the great master of wet road racing, was an unassailable winner in the rain with his great white Mercedes-Benz.

The voiturettes

In vintage days the 'second formula' below the Grands Prix was the voiturette or light car class. This admitted cars of up to 1,500cc from 1920 to 1925, sometimes with 1,100cc and 750cc sub-classes, but when the Grand Prix Formula was reduced to 1,500cc in 1926–27 Continental voiturette races were restricted to 1,100cc cars.

At first the small 16-valve four-cylinder Bugatti was the most successful voiturette, winning races at Le Mans in 1920 and Brescia and Barcelona in 1921. Meantime the Sunbeam-Talbot-Darracq combine hit on the idea of using half their 3 litre straight-eight twin camshaft Grand Prix engine in a smaller chassis, and the pretty little Talbot-Darracqs that appeared in mid-1921 never lost a voiturette race from then until 1926. This one-make domination rather discouraged the opposition, and the only worthy adversaries to the Talbots, the 1½ litre four cylinder Fiats, never met them in a race.

The supplementary 1,100cc category was dominated by the twin overhead camshaft Salmsons, while

Scenes from the classics. Above: *the start at Le Mans, 1926, with OM No.19 and Bentley No.7 getting away. The British car had the lead 20 minutes from the end of the 24 hours when it slid off-course. The same car with the same drivers, Davis and Benjafield, won in 1927. Left: the 1923 Le Mans winner, the Lagache/Leonard 3 litre Chenard-Walcker, cornering at Pontlieue.*

Below: *Earl Howe's vast 7 litre Mercedes-Benz about to gobble up racing motorcyclist Vic Horsman's tiny 750cc Triumph in the 1930 Ulster TT. Horsman's passenger is practising sidecar racing tactics!*

where there was a 750cc class the little Austin Seven invariably shone. An important new British race was the 200 Miles Race, inaugurated in 1921 on the Brooklands outer circuit. The Talbots won every year up to 1926 (except 1923 when they non-started and Alvis took the honours). The '200' deteriorated in its later vintage years, Malcolm Campbell winning in 1927 with a Bugatti and in 1928 with a Delage.

The Continental step-down from 1,500 to 1,100cc in 1926 gave the French Amilcar team their chance. Their beautiful miniature Grand Prix car with supercharged six-cylinder engine proved as invincible as the bigger contemporary Delages, despite Salmson efforts to stop them with a remarkable blown 1,100cc straight-eight with desmodromic valves. In fact, so fast was the Amilcar six that it continued winning voiturette races until well in the 1930s.

Track racing

After Duesenberg's unexpected win in the 1921 French Grand Prix, the Americans unfortunately stayed aloof from European-style racing, being quite content with their annual Indianapolis 500 Miles Race on the famous 2½ mile oblong track with its four banked corners, together with many lesser track races. Main contenders were Duesenberg and Miller, with very high-efficiency straight-eight engines, both with centrifugal supercharging. These proved extremely fast – the Americans were well ahead of Europe both in high speed engine development and in single-seater body design at that time, and a 1½ litre Miller actually exceeded 164mph on the Muroc dried lake bed in 1927.

Millers won Indianapolis in 1923, 1926, 1928, 1929 and 1930; Duesenbergs won in 1924, 1925 and 1927, while the 1922 winner had a Duesenberg engine in a Miller chassis. The highest average of the decade was de Paolo's 101·13mph in 1925 with a 2 litre car. Examples of one or other make crossed the Atlantic to race against the Europeans at Monza, with but small success, while European cars such as 2 litre Bugatti, Mercedes and Fiat, 1½ litre Grand Prix Delage and 16-cylinder Maserati tackled Indianapolis in return, but were no match for the home cars.

Track racing in Europe was never so popular as in the USA, although England had Brooklands where regular race meetings and many record attempts were held. The 2¾-mile banked track was invaluable for car testing and development, although its prewar smoothness had suffered during the 1914–18 War. Perhaps because of the success of the 200 Miles Race in 1921, there were exciting proposals in 1922 to hold a 500 Miles Race for Grand Prix type cars at Brooklands, but nothing came of this.

Seven years later, however, such an event for unlimited racing cars actually took place on the outer circuit. To accommodate five capacity classes from under 1,100cc to over 5,000cc a handicap system of time allowances was employed, but on a dry track nothing could restrain two Bentleys, a 4½ litre winning at 107·32mph. This was faster than any Indianapolis 500-winning speed then, although no Ameri-

The first and so far only all-American combination to win the French Grand Prix – Jimmy Murphy and mechanic Ernie Olsen in the left-hand-drive 3 litre straight-eight Duesenberg, winners in 1921 despite an empty radiator and a punctured rear tyre (clearly visible here), both caused by stones on the unmetalled circuit at Le Mans.

can cars were larger than 2 litres. The 1930 Brooklands '500' showed the adverse side of the handicapping system so beloved by the British. It rained, slowing the fastest cars, and a 747cc blown Austin Seven won on handicap at 83·41mph, whereas the blown 4½ litre Bentley which came second averaged 112·12mph. It was a creditable run by the tiny Austin, but it was ludicrous that such a car won "the fastest race in the world".

Not that 500 Miles race-winning averages approached the full potential speeds at Brooklands. In 1922 K. Lee Guinness with a large aero-engined Sunbeam had lapped the outer circuit at 123·39mph, and by 1925 Parry Thomas had lapped at 129·36mph in his Leyland-Thomas. At the end of the decade the lap

One of America's greatest drivers of the 1920s was Frank Lockhart, winner of the 1926 Indianapolis '500' in this 1½ litre supercharged eight-cylinder Miller '91' at 94·63 mph, despite rain which stopped the race at 400 miles.

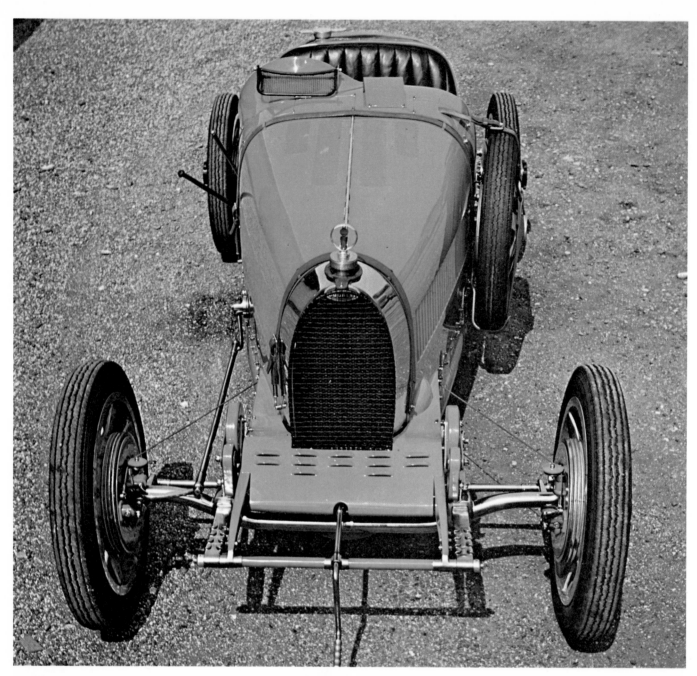

record stood to Kaye Don in a 4 litre 12-cylinder Sunbeam at 137·58mph, whereas the fastest Indianapolis lap then stood at 124·018mph, set by Leon Duray on a 1½ litre Miller while qualifying in 1928.

On the Continent Brooklands-type banked tracks were created, with mixed success. The Spanish Sitges circuit was built near Barcelona in 1923, but after a few races it was abandoned as dangerous, for the banking angles had been miscalculated. The French opened the combined road and track at Montlhéry, near Paris, in 1924, its banked *piste de vitesse*, shorter and smoother than Brooklands, becoming a popular venue for record breaking. Another French track was opened at Miramas, inland of Marseilles, that same year, but it proved far too rough, and remote, and was never a success.

Fastest on earth

The prestige of breaking the Land Speed Record has ensured a flow of special cars and drivers ever since the first figure of 39·24mph was set in 1898. At the War's end the official record stood to the English driver Hornsted in a German 21½ litre Benz at 124·10mph, set at Brooklands in 1914. This modest speed had, in fact, twice been bettered one-way by a 200hp Blitzen Benz in America, back in 1910 and 1911, but the Paris ruling body insisted on two-way runs, with the mean speed as the record, and, moreover, refused to accept any American claims, declaring them unofficial!

Thus two one-way claims from the USA, by de Palma's V12 Packard at 149·875mph in 1919, and by Milton's twin-engined Duesenberg at 156·03mph in 1920, were discounted, while Hornsted's 1914 record lived on.

With so many redundant aircraft engines around after the War, it was natural in an 'anything goes' contest like being fastest on earth that such engines, sold at scrap prices, would be persuaded into reinforced chassis. In 1922 K. Lee Guinness (the man who launched the KLG plug) turned out at Brooklands with a big Sunbeam racing car powered by an 18·3 litre 12-cylinder 'Manitou' aero-engine, and clocked a mean speed of 133.75mph – the first post-War record, but the last ever made at Brooklands, which was now too short for such high speeds.

Two years later two great cars faced each other at a spring meeting on the Arpajon road outside Paris. One was a 10½ litre V12 Delage driven by Frenchman René Thomas; the other was a ferocious chain-driven Fiat special with 21·7 litre six-cylinder aero-engine, built and driven by Englishman Ernest Eldridge. Thomas went first, and broke Guinness' record at 143·31mph. Eldridge countered with 146·8mph, whereupon Thomas protested that the Fiat lacked a proper reverse as required by the rules. Eldridge took his car away, devised a reverse and was back six days later – and this time he took the record officially at 146·01mph.

But not for long. Two months later Malcolm Campbell, inveterate British record collector who eventually broke the 'world's fastest' nine times, took his first at 146·16mph on Pendine sands, Wales,

Ever revered for its superb shape, let alone its racing achievements, is the Type 35 straight-eight Bugatti, deemed by many to represent the classic vintage racing car at its most sublime. Constructional features such as the exquisite 'horseshoe' radiator which tapers with the bodywork, the deceptively delicate looking front axle, the cast aluminium wheels, the sculptured cylinder block and the impeccable proportions raise the GP Bugatti from a mere mechanical device to sheer artistry in metal. It is highly unlikely that any Type 35 in the 1920s ever gleamed so resplendently as this somewhat over-restored example.

Below: *not every Bugatti was so small and jewel-like. At the extreme opposite was the Type 41 Royale of 1927–1933, with its immense 12·7 litre 300bhp straight-eight engine able to run at 3mph in top gear. Wheelbase alone was 14ft 1in, and weight was 2¾ tons. This beautiful cabriolet was bodied by Weinberger of Munich.*

The heyday of British hillclimbing was in the early 1920s.
Above: one of the great gradient artists of those carefree
days, Archie Frazer Nash, in spectacular action with
his famous twin-cylinder GN 'Kim', at Shelsley Walsh,
1921.

Below: massed spectators watch a competitor storm up
Kop, the hill where in 1925 an accident precipitated the
ban on all racing over British public roads.
Bottom: after the Kop accident, Shelsley Walsh on private
ground assumed greater importance. C.M. Harvey in a
front drive 1½ litre Alvis on the famous hill in 1926.

in the ex-Guinness 350hp Sunbeam which he called
'Bluebird'. With the same car further streamlined he
improved to 150·76mph in 1925, only to lose the
honour the following year to a highly tuned 4 litre
V12 road racing Sunbeam, driven at 152·33mph by
Henry Segrave on Southport sands. That was the last
road-racing type car to break the record; thereafter
all were vast-engined monsters.

The record next fell to the popular Welsh driver
Parry Thomas with his 26·9 litre Liberty-engined
'Babs', doing 169·30mph at Pendine one day in 1926,
and 171·02mph the next. Campbell replied with an
all-new 'Bluebird' powered by a 22·3 litre Napier
Lion, beating 'Babs' at 174·883mph early in 1927.
Tragedy ensued, for during his return attempt
Thomas's car slewed off-course, then rolled over.
Poor Thomas died at once from head injuries, while
the wreck of 'Babs' was buried in Pendine sands until
1970, when Owen Wyn Owen from Bangor obtained
permission to dig it up for restoration.

The next goal, 200mph, was reached by Segrave
at Daytona, Florida, with the stupendous twin-
engined 1,000hp Sunbeam in 1927. His 203·792mph
record stood for almost a year, when Campbell
managed 206·956mph – only to meet unexpected
American opposition at Daytona from two vastly
differing cars. One was Ray Keech's huge, crude
White Triplex with *three* Liberty engines, which took
Campbell's record by less than 1mph; the other was
Lockhart's exquisite little 3 litre 16 cylinder Stutz
Black Hawk, which burst a tyre at over 200mph and
crashed, its luckless driver being thrown out and
killed.

In 1929 Segrave took a sophisticated new car, the
Napier Lion-engined 'Golden Arrow', to Daytona and
raised the record to 231·446mph with insolent ease,
and this was to stand until 1931. It was challenged
the following day by the Triplex. Unfortunately this

The land speed record drew some notable contenders in Vintage days. Capt (later Sir) Malcolm Campbell, who broke it nine times between 1924 and 1935, is seen (above) in 1927 with his Napier-engined Bluebird at Pendine, South Wales, where despite the wet beach he clocked 174·883mph.

Right: Attacking Campbell's record, the popular Welsh driver Parry Thomas (here in his track Leyland-Thomas in the Boulogne speed trials) was killed when his Liberty-engined 'Babs' car went out of control.

Below: Henry Segrave broke the 200mph barrier, averaging 203·79mph with this massive twin-engined 1000hp Sunbeam.

Racing cars of the 1920s are regularly exercised in Britain at VSCC race meetings today; here at Silverstone are the 4 litre V12 Sunbeam, two Bugattis and the 10½ litre V12 Delage in 1927.

plucky attempt brought a third land speed record fatality when the driver, Lee Bible, lost control and was killed. In a decade the record had risen from 124mph to over 231mph, thanks to sheer brute power. The cars were fascinating freaks, contributing little or nothing to car design, yet such is the challenge, that many more, with far more power, were to come in future years.

Reliving the Vintage era

It is interesting that four of these historic land speed record breakers – the 350hp Sunbeam of 1922, the 10½ litre 12 cylinder Delage and 21·7 litre Fiat which duelled at Arpajon in 1924, and the 4 litre V12 Sunbeam of 1926 – have all been seen in action in recent years racing on British circuits. This is entirely due to the enterprise of the Vintage Sports Car Club in organising regular race meetings for vintage sports and racing cars. These began before the Second World War and have enlivened the British calendar ever since, at circuits including Silverstone, Goodwood, Oulton Park, Castle Combe and Thruxton.

They have enabled vintage enthusiasts to see, hear – and smell! – the classic Bugattis, Delages, Sunbeams and Alfa Romeos of bygone Grands Prix in full and stirring action, the glorious Bentleys, historic 1,100cc Amilcar sixes, GNs and Frazer Nashes, Alvises, Vauxhalls, Rileys, Lea-Francises, Lagondas etc, not only in vintage racing but rallies and driving tests too. One wonders how many such cars could be seen today but for the VSCC, which, in catering for its own interests almost 40 years ago, launched the Vintage movement on the motoring world.

Their original members drove vintage sports cars, such as Alvises, Bentleys, Bugattis, Rileys and Salmsons, in plain preference to the offerings of the mid-1930s, such as oil-drinking, pseudo-sports Wolseley Hornet sixes, the M.G.s and Singers with their Le Mans 'uniform' – slab rear tanks, wind cowls, stone-guards, sporty wings and strapped twin spare wheels – the handsome but non-performing Avon Standards, and other variations on the quantity-production theme.

Interest in the vintage car began to widen beyond the Club during the Second World War, when no new cars at all were being built, and those of the 1920s manifestly lasted better than newer ones. Who can say how many vintage models were spared death as metal salvage, or escaped the post-war breakers' yards as a result of VSCC influence? Priceless relics have been saved, and impeccably restored, and motoring history made richer thereby.

Since then the Vintage movement has grown ever larger, many one-make clubs and registers have been formed, and there are speed hillclimbs, historic parades, rallies and concours d'elegance at home and overseas to further spread the interest. All who love vintage cars owe a debt to the VSCC.

Perhaps I may end on a lighthearted note, with that priceless poem by the 'motoring muse', the late W.H. Charnock, which so recaptures the spirit of the movement. It is entitled "Vintage Brotherhood" and is reproduced by courtesy of Villiers Publications Ltd.:

We are the Vintage brotherhood, our cars are very old,
Each thing sits in its proper place and we sit in the cold,
Conducting our machinery behind an aero screen,
While little boys cry 'Racer' and the moderns wax
obscene.

Our cars may make more noise than theirs, they may
not go as fast,
They've no push-button radio, but heavens how they
last,
These, then, our loved and trusted friends, of more than
human worth,
For craftsmanship and character, the greatest things
on earth.

The Aston is a gentleman, this no one will deny,
His copious oil is ever cool, his well-cut gears are high,
He shares, with lean Lagonda, that secret of the past,
Of how to wear a cycle wing, and how to make it last.

The Bentley is a jovial chap, his lines are sleek and
  pleasant,
He trumpets gaily down the road, a two-ton
  adolescent,
But when at rest his water pump weeps hot nostalgic
  tears,
Remembering the glories of those green and bygone
  years.

The Talbot's an eccentric type, tied up in metric thread,
You take her body off before you can detach her head,
And if you wish to drop the sump, rear axle first
  remove,
Oh, how the Talboteers must work if they would gain
  her love.

Patrician 30/98, all lesser types atop,
No doubt because he's never known just how and when
  to stop,
The sane and simple Alvis, with a rabbit on the rad,
The Austin Seven ever making modern motors mad.

The Merc. with outside plumbing like the Corporation
  drains,
The Frazer Nash who strews our roads with little bits
  of chains,
Old Bullnose and Two-lunger, those maids of work for
  all,
The Riley, Leaf and Lambda — their charms shall never
  pall.

We are the Vintage brotherhood, our cars are hell to run,
The moderns get the spares they need, but we get all the
  fun,
No hydramatic nonsense, no bulbous tin for us —
And if you break a crankshaft you can always take a
  bus.

Racing conditions in the Vintage years differed greatly
from those of today. Above: the field for the 1925 200
Miles Race spread itself comfortably over the broad but
bumpy concrete of Brooklands track in Surrey.

Below: the unique Monaco 'round the houses' Grand Prix
through the narrow confines of Monte Carlo city, was
inaugurated in 1929, when the Bugattis and their rivals
had to race over tramlines.

VINTAGE MILESTONES

1919

Servo-assisted four-wheel brakes (Hispano-Suiza, France)

First production straight-eight (Isotta-Fraschini, Italy)

First all-aluminium engine with wet cylinder liners (AC, Britain)

1920

Hydraulically-operated four-wheel brakes (Duesenberg, USA)

First use of torsion bars in suspension (Leyland, Britain)

1921

All-independent suspension (Sizaire-Frères, France)

1922

Unitary chassis/body construction, independent front suspension and V4 engine (Lancia Lambda, Italy)

Austin Seven 'baby' car with four wheel brakes introduced (Britain)

First electric screen wipers (Trico, USA)

Backbone-framed, rear engined, all-independently sprung light car (San Giusto, Italy)

Mercedes market first supercharged cars in Europe (Germany)

1923

Ethyl leaded fuels introduced (USA)

1924

First quantity-production all-steel saloon body (Dodge, USA)

Rear-engined Benz sports car with rear swing axles and inboard brakes introduced (Germany)

Introduction of Duco quick-drying cellulose lacquer by Du Pont (USA)

1925

Weymann fabric-covered, flexible wood body structure introduced.

The first production British car with hydraulic brakes (Triumph 13–35)

Bosch introduce electric direction indicators (Germany)

1926

Silentbloc oil-less rubber-bushed bearings introduced.

Front-wheel-drive Tracta introduced (France)

First traffic signals in London (at top of St. James Street)

First 'Keep Left' sign, Hyde Park Corner.

1927

Studebaker and Oldsmobile pioneer use of chromium plating (USA)

Mid-engined, all independently sprung, streamlined saloon built by Claveau (France)

1928

Unbreakable safety glass introduced (USA)

Cadillac introduce synchromesh gears (called 'clashless')

Front-wheel-drive Alvis introduced (Britain)

1929

Chrysler pioneer rustproofing of car bodies (USA)

Ruxton and Cord front-drive models introduced (USA)

1930

Cadillac market first production V-16 cylinder car (USA)

Studebaker adopt thin-wall engine bearings (USA).

Overleaf: *And so, with cars like this transitional Model A Ford, the Vintage decade gave way to the '30s, and many cars became cheaper, duller and often nastier; an era had ended.*

INDEX